GLOBAL ENTREPRENEURSHIP: ANALYSES OF PERFORMANCE AND CHALLENGES

BUSINESS ISSUES, COMPETITION AND ENTREPRENEURSHIP

Additional books in this series can be found on Nova's website under the Series tab.

Additional E-books in this series can be found on Nova's website under the E-books tab.

GLOBAL ENTREPRENEURSHIP: ANALYSES OF PERFORMANCE AND CHALLENGES

STEPHEN M. RICE

AND

JACLYN L. STEINER

EDITORS

Nova Science Publishers, Inc.

New York

LIBRARY OF CONGRESS CATALOGING-IN-PUBLICATION DATA

Global entrepreneurship : analyses of performance and challenges / editors,
Stephen M. Rice and Jaclyn L. Steiner.
p. cm.
  Includes bibliographical references and index.
  ISBN 978-1-61209-556-1 (hbk. : alk. paper)
  1. Entrepreneurship. 2. Entrepreneurship--United States. 3. New business
enterprises. 4. New business enterprises--United States. 5. Small
business. 6. Small business--United States. I. Rice, Stephen M. II.
Steiner, Jaclyn L.
  HB615.G584 2011
  338'.04--dc22
2011004008

Published by Nova Science Publishers, Inc. † *New York*

CONTENTS

Preface   **vii**

Chapter 1   Global Entrepreneurship and the United States   **1**
Zoltan J. Acs and Laszlo Szerb

Chapter 2   The Impact of International Competition
on Small-Firm Exit in U.S. Manufacturing   **57**
Robert M. Feinberg

Chapter 3   Looking Ahead: Opportunities and Challenges
for Entrepreneurship and Small Business Owners   **79**
Chad Moutray

Chapter Sources   **101**

Index   **103**

PREFACE

The United States appears among the top entrepreneurial economies and ranks third on the GEDI. It performs very well on the aspirations sub-index but lags somewhat on the attitudes and activity sub-indexes. This new book examines the performance of the United States on the Global Entrepreneurship and Development Index (GEDI), which captures the contextual features of entrepreneurship

Chapter 1- This paper looks at the performance of the United States on the Global Entrepreneurship and Development Index (GEDI), which captures the contextual features of entrepreneurship. The index builds on and improves earlier measures by capturing quantitative and qualitative aspects of entrepreneurship. It measures entrepreneurial performance in 71 countries over three sub-indexes, 14 pillars, and 31 individual and institutional variables. The United States appears among the top entrepreneurial economies and ranks third on the GEDI. It performs very well on the aspirations subindex but lags somewhat on the attitudes and activity sub-indexes. At the pillar level, the United States is strong in startup skills, competition, and new technology but weak in cultural support, tech sector, and high-growth business. U.S. performance appears be stronger on institutional variables than on individual variables. The United States' apparent weakness in the tech sector and its lack of cultural support for entrepreneurship, coupled with lack of high-growth business can be traced to a number of sources. Chief among these are the changing political environment and international volatility, the bursting of the tech sector bubble of the 1990s, the recent recession, and the improving performance of other counties. However, despite some drawbacks, U.S. performance on the index remains strong.

Chapter 2- This econometric study uses Statistics of U.S. Businesses (SUSB) data to examine the impact of trade on small manufacturers. As global trade increases and currency exchange rates fluctuate, concerns about their impact on small U.S. manufacturers increase. Small manufacturers, by the nature of their scale of operations, are less able to insulate themselves from foreign competition than large manufacturers. Although not without costs, large manufacturers have greater leeway in managing the effects of international competition: they can move production offshore, sign long-term commodity contracts in foreign currencies, or use other tactics to weather global shifts.

Chapter 3- Small businesses continue to struggle in the economic downturn, and it will be important for policy leaders to get the economy moving again. Small businesses will be a large part of that, as entrepreneurs will spur new innovation and employment in the coming years. These firms will continue to be the job- generators that we have become accustomed to. With that said, industries will recover from the downturn in different ways, and some industries have clearly been hit harder this time than in past business cycles.

In: Global Entrepreneurship   ISBN: 978-1-61209-556-1
Editors: S. M. Rice and J. L. Steiner   © 2011 Nova Science Publishers, Inc.

Chapter 1

GLOBAL ENTREPRENEURSHIP AND THE UNITED STATES

Zoltan J. Acs and Laszlo Szerb

1. EXECUTIVE SUMMARY

This paper looks at the performance of the United States on the Global Entrepreneurship and Development Index (GEDI), which captures the contextual features of entrepreneurship. The index builds on and improves earlier measures by capturing quantitative and qualitative aspects of entrepreneurship. It measures entrepreneurial performance in 71 countries over three sub-indexes, 14 pillars, and 31 individual and institutional variables. The United States appears among the top entrepreneurial economies and ranks third on the GEDI. It performs very well on the aspirations subindex but lags somewhat on the attitudes and activity sub-indexes. At the pillar level, the United States is strong in startup skills, competition, and new technology but weak in cultural support, tech sector, and high-growth business. U.S. performance appears be stronger on institutional variables than on individual variables. The United States' apparent weakness in the tech sector and its lack of cultural support for entrepreneurship, coupled with lack of high-growth business can be traced to a number of sources. Chief among these are the changing political environment and international volatility, the bursting of the tech sector bubble of the 1990s, the recent recession, and the improving performance of other counties. However, despite some drawbacks, U.S. performance on the index remains strong.

2. INTRODUCTION

While small businesses and entrepreneurship are different, the two concepts are frequently used interchangeably.[1] Since entrepreneurship is often observed in small and new businesses the analysis of these concepts overlaps, causing fundamental problems. A misbegotten conclusion of this jumbling is to equate the increasing number of businesses with the enhancement of entrepreneurship. In fact, decreasing unemployment and job creation cannot be expected to flow from the creation of numerous tiny businesses; they are instead the result of a small number of extraordinary high-growth entrepreneurial ventures, called "gazelles."[2] At the outset of this paper, we would like to clearly make thedistinction that small business is basically a quantitative activity, and entrepreneurship is a qualitative phenomenon.

2.1. Assessing Entrepreneurship

For a long time, the level of entrepreneurship has been evaluated by some quantitative measure, for instance the self-employment rate, business ownership rate, or business startups.[3] Over the last decade, the Global Entrepreneurship Monitor's Total Early-stage Entrepreneurial Activity (TEA)[4] ratio has become a widely used measure of entrepreneurship. While these indicators or ratios have undergone some modification and change to incorporate *qualitative* measures, like education and high growth firms, they are basically limited to measuring the *quantity* of existing or nascent businesses.[5] There are five major shortcomings with these attempts at measuring entrepreneurship:

1. While all the definitions emphasize the multifaceted nature of entrepreneurship— including innovation, risk taking, opportunity recognition, high-growth opportunity motivations, and unusual "judgmental" decision-making, they measure only one, and perhaps not even the most important, aspect of entrepreneurship. [6]

2. The indexes fail to incorporate the businesses' differing impacts; a traditional agricultural business established in Uganda or Peru is given equal importance as an Internet-related venture in Silicon Valley.
3. The most entrepreneurial nations are defined as those having the largest number of businesses. These are generally the developing countries of Africa or South America.[7]
4. These measures do not take into account differences in environmental factors. In fact, the efficiency and sophistication of the institutional setting could have a major influence on the quality of entrepreneurship.
5. Since self-employment and the business ownership ratio decline as a country develops, indexes that rely on them appear to show that higher levels of development are associated with decreasing levels of entrepreneurship. This phenomenon is inconsistent with mainstream economic theories which posit a direct connection between entrepreneurship and development.

This kind of index would give policymakers false guidance, putting the focus on increasing the quantity of entrepreneurship, when quality is of greater import.

Recent efforts of the OECD and European Union have aimed to provide a sophisticated measure of entrepreneurship encompassing three broad areas: *the determinants of entrepreneurship* (regulation, R&D, entrepreneurial capabilities, culture, access to finance and market conditions); *entrepreneurial performance* (firms, employment, and wealth); and *the impact of entrepreneurship*. While the first two publications of the OECD's Entrepreneurship Indicator Program[8] contain many entrepreneurship-related data and indicators, a more highly evolved measure of entrepreneurship is still missing.

The shortcomings of previous entrepreneurship indicators and the need to clarify the role of entrepreneurship in economic development were the two major reasons underlying the creation of the Acs-Szerb Global Entrepreneurship and Development Index (GEDI). [9] At present, this is the only index to fulfill the three major requirements of entrepreneurship index building, namely,

1. Sufficient complexity to capture the multidimensional nature of entrepreneurship;

2. Inclusion of indicators encompassing quality-related differences, in addition to quantitative or level-related measures; and
3. Inclusion of individual-level as well as institutional variables.

Unlike other entrepreneurship indexes the relationship between the GEDI and economic development appears to be mildly S-shaped, implying a positive relationship between entrepreneurship and economic development.[10] Therefore the GEDI is a proper tool to provide policy suggestions to increase economic development via entrepreneurship enhancement. Since economic growth is ultimately the result of many factors in addition to entrepreneurship, the GEDI can explain only a part of short-term economic growth.

2.2. Stages of Development

In his classic text W.W. Rostow (1960) suggested that countries go through five stages of economic growth. Michael Porter (2002) has provided a modern rendition of Rostow's typology by identifying three stages of development (as opposed to growth). Porter identifies a factor-driven stage, an efficiency-driven stage, and an innovation-driven stage, and he adds two transitions. While Rostow focused on the age of high mass consumption, Porter's model encompasses recent developments in the economics of knowledge, hence he focuses on the innovation. Historically, an elite entrepreneurial class appears to have played a leading role in innovation and economic development.

The factor-driven stage is marked by high rates of agricultural self-employment. Countries in this stage compete through low-cost efficiencies in the production of commodities or low value-added products. Sole proprietor-ships—i.e., the selfemployed—probably account for most small manufacturing firms and service firms.

Almost all economies experience this stage of economic development. These countries neither create knowledge for innovation nor use knowledge for exporting.

To compete in the efficiency-driven stage, countries must have efficient productive practices in large markets, which allow companies to exploit economies of scale. Industries in this stage are manufacturers that provide basic services. The efficiency- driven stage is marked by decreasing rates of self-employment. When capital and labor are substitutes, an increase in the capital stock increases returns from working and lowers returns from managing.

The innovation-driven stage is marked by an increase in knowledge-intensive activities (Romer 1990). In the innovation-driven stage knowledge provides the key input. In this stage the focus shifts from firms to agents in possession of new knowledge (Acs et al 2009). The agent decides to start a new firm based on expected net returns from a new product. The innovation-driven stage is biased towards high value added industries in which entrepreneurial activity is important.

According to Sala-I-Martin et al (2007) the first two stages of development are dominated by institutions. In fact, innovation accounts for only about 5 percent of economic activity in factor-driven economies and rises to 10 percent in the efficiency driven stage. However, in the innovation-driven stage when opportunities for productivity gains from factors and efficiency have been exhausted, innovation accounts for 30 percent of economic activity.

We see an S-shaped relationship between entrepreneurship and economic development because in the first transition stage entrepreneurship plays a role but it increases at a decreasing rate as the efficiency stage takes over. However, as we move from the efficiency-driven stage to the innovation driven stage (the knowledge-driven stage) entrepreneurship plays a more important role increasing at an increasing rate and latter at a decreasing rate (Figure 1).

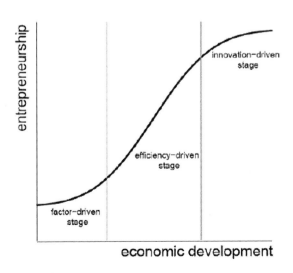

Figure 1. Entrepreneurship and Stages of Economic Development

2.3. Purpose and Structure

The basic aim of this chapter is to present and analyze U.S. entrepreneurial performance with the help of the Global Entrepreneurship and Development Index. The analysis includes an in-depth investigation of the GEDI's component sub-indexes, pillars, and variables. The change in the three sub-indexes over the 2006-2009 time period is also shown. We compare the United States to the leading economies and to other transitional or rapidly emerging nations. We also explore the United States's strengths and weaknesses as revealed by the index. In so doing, we attempt to provide tailor-made policy guidance on how to improve U.S. entrepreneurial performance, and with it, economic development. As mentioned earlier such improvement cannot be achieved by increasing the number of startups by any means. The United States does not simply need more new businesses; it needs more highly productive ventures. A potential way of achieving this kind of productivity improvement is to make progress in entrepreneurship. The report proceeds as follows: As a starting point, the basic description of the Global Entrepreneurship and Development Index is provided in section 2. Section 3 contains an investigation of the entrepreneurial position of the United States based on the GEDI and the three sub-indexes. Sections 4 and 5 provide an in-depth examination of the U.S. position at the pillar and the variable level, respectively. Finally Section 6 provides tailor- made public policy suggestions on how to improve the United States's entrepreneurial position.

3. THE GLOBAL ENTREPRENEURSHIP AND DEVELOPMENT INDEX

Entrepreneurship is a complex creature which consists of numerous dimensions. It is distinct from small businesses, self-employment, craftsmanship, and usual businesses; it is not associated as a phenomenon with buyouts, change of ownership, or management succession. In light of the relevance of entrepreneurship to generating economic growth, one needs to get down to brass tacks in terms of finding a suitable measure or indicator for the level of entrepreneurship in an economy before embarking on policy initiatives. A number of attempts have been made in this respect to collect the relevant data and find suitable proxies for entrepreneurship (see for example

Acs, Audretsch and Evans 1994; Blanchflower 2000; Blanchflower et al.2001; Grilo and Thurik 2008; Román 2006).

Since its inception in 1999, the Global Entrepreneurship Monitor (GEM) research consortium has worked to measure and to compare entrepreneurial activity across countries. The best known entrepreneurship measure used by GEM researchers is the Total Early-phase Entrepreneurial Activity (TEA) index. However, the TEA index's usefulness as a measure of entrepreneurship has several limitations for cross-country comparisons (Hindle, 2006). Others have criticized the TEA for not capturing entrepreneurship in existing businesses, data inconsistency, and conflicting interpretations of the questions from one country to the next (Audretsch 2002, OECD 2006, Baumol et al. 2007, Godin et al. 2008).

Over the past decade, the contextual setting of entrepreneurship has received increasing attention. The widely applied indicators of entrepreneurship (self-employment, TEA, new venture creation) focus purely on individual or firm-level aggregates, failing to suitably account for the quality of the (institutional) environment. The Ease of Doing Business index, the Global Competitiveness Index, and the Index of Economic Freedom try to capture the institutional features of the participating countries (Djankov et al 2002, Miller and Holmes 2010, Sala-I-Martin et al. 2007; Porter and Schwab, 2008; Porter et al. 2007). At the same time in the context of entrepreneurship, while institutions are vital for development they provide only a part of the picture. The most important drawback of these indexes is their lack of microeconomic foundation.

From an examination of a vast pool of entrepreneurship-related data collected across countries, time periods, and surveys, one finds that a comprehensive, uniformly accepted, regularly assessed data gathering effort for entrepreneurship does not exist yet. We agree with Ahmad and Hoffman (2007) that none of the existing measures fully captures the essence of entrepreneurship, empirically or conceptually.

To this end, we create an independent index to provide a comprehensive measure of entrepreneurship. The index draws on previous measures of economic freedom, competitiveness, and entrepreneurial activity but improves on each of these by providing a more focused and quality-oriented approach (Acemoglu and Johnson, 2005; Acemoglu, Johnson and Robinson, 2001).

3.1. The Sub-Indexes

For the purposes of this paper, entrepreneurship is defined as *a dynamic interaction of attitudes, activities, and aspirations that vary across stages of economic development.* This approach is consistent with the revised version of the GEM conceptual model (Bosma et al. 2009). The process of building our index consists of (1) selection of variables and weights, (2) calculation of pillars, (3) generation of sub-indexes, and finally, (4) creation of the super-index. Data for the individual-level variables in the index comes from the GEM annual adult population surveys. A description of the individual variables is provided in Appendix Table A.1. Since GEM lacks the necessary institutional weighting variables, we make use of other widely used relevant data. A description of the institutional variables and their respective data sources is provided in Appendix Table A.2. The variables are used to construct the 14 pillars which then go into the construction of the three sub-indexes. The three sub-indexes of activity, aspiration, and attitudes combine to constitute the entrepreneurship super-index, which we call the Global Entrepreneurship and Development Index (GEDI). Figure 2 contains a schematic diagram of the index's components.

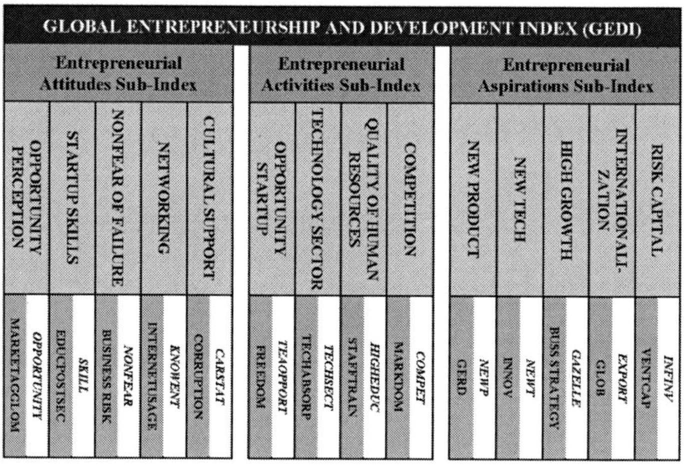

GLOBAL ENTREPRENEURSHIP AND DEVELOPMENT INDEX (GEDI)

Entrepreneurial Attitudes Sub-Index					Entrepreneurial Activities Sub-Index				Entrepreneurial Aspirations Sub-Index				
OPPORTUNITY PERCEPTION	STARTUP SKILLS	NONFEAR OF FAILURE	NETWORKING	CULTURAL SUPPORT	OPPORTUNITY STARTUP	TECHNOLOGY SECTOR	QUALITY OF HUMAN RESOURCES	COMPETITION	NEW PRODUCT	NEW TECH	HIGH GROWTH	INTERNATIONALI-ZATION	RISK CAPITAL
MARKETAGGLOM / OPPORTUNITY	EDUCPOSTSEC / SKILL	BUSINESS RISK / NONFEAR	INTERNETUSAGE / KNOWENT	CORRUPTION / CARSTAT	FREEDOM / TEAOPPORT	TECHABSORP / TECHSECT	STAFFTRAIN / HIGHEDUC	MARKDOM / COMPET	GERD / NEWP	INNOV / NEWT	BUSS STRATEGY / GAZELLE	GLOB / EXPORT	VENTCAP / INFINV

Note: The GEDI is a super-index made up of three sub-indexes, each of which is composed of several pillars. Each pillar consists of an institutional variable (denoted in bold) and an individual variable (denoted in bold italic). The data values for each variable are gathered from wide ranging sources.

Figure 2. Structure of the Global Entrepreneurship and Development Index (GEDI)

For the first sub-index, entrepreneurial attitudes are defined as the general disposition of a country's population toward entrepreneurs, entrepreneurship, and business start-ups. The index involves measures for the population's opportunity perception potential, the perceived startup skills, feel of fear of failure, networking prospects, and cultural respect for the entrepreneur. Among the pillars that make up the index, the population's capacity for opportunity perception is seen to be an essential ingredient of entrepreneurial startups (Sørensen and Sorenson 2003). Successful venture launching requires the potential entrepreneur to have the necessary level of startup skills (Papagiannidis and Li 2005). Among the personal entrepreneurial traits, fear of failure is one of the most important obstacles hindering startups (Caliendo, Fossen and Kritikos 2009, Wagner 2002). Better networked entrepreneurs are more successful, can identify more viable opportunities, and gain access to more and better resources (Minniti 2005, Shane and Cable 2003). And without strong cultural support, the best and the brightest individuals do not want to be entrepreneurs and decide to enter some other profession (Davidsson, 2004; Guiso et al. 2006). Moreover, culture can even influence entrepreneurial potential and traits (Mueller and Thomas 2001).

For the second sub-index, *entrepreneurial activity* is defined as the startup activity in the medium- or high-technology sector initiated by educated entrepreneurs in response to business opportunities in a somewhat competitive environment. The choice of indicators used to build this sub-index reflects the belief that opportunity entrepreneurs are better prepared, possess superior skills, and earn more than necessity entrepreneurs (Bhola et al. 2006; Block and Wagner 2006). Operating in the technology sector is important, as high rates of startups in most factor-driven countries are mainly in the traditional sectors and do not represent high potential (Acs and Varga 2005). The entrepreneur's level of education is another important feature of a venture with high growth potential (Bates 1990). And cut-throat competition may hinder business existence and growth, so a lower number of competitors improves chances of survival, as well as future development prospects (Baumol, Litan, and Schramm 2007).

The third sub-index, *entrepreneurial aspiration,* is defined as the efforts of the early- stage entrepreneur to introduce new products and services, develop new production processes, penetrate foreign markets, substantially increase the number of firm employees, and finance the business with either formal or informal venture capital, or both. Product and process innovation, internationalization, as well as high growth are included in the measure. The capability to produce or sell products that customers consider to be new is one of Schumpeter's forms of creating "new combinations" (Schumpeter 1934). Applying or creating new technology and production processes is another important feature of businesses with high growth potential (Acs and Varga 2005). The role of "gazelles" or high-growth businesses is vital, and several empirical studies (Autio 2007) support David Birch's 1994 finding that only a few businesses, perhaps 2-4 percent, are responsible for the vast majority of new job creation (60-80 percent). Internationalization is believed to be a major determinant of growth (De Clercq, Sapienza, and Crijns 2005). Finally the availability of risk finance, in particular equity rather than debt, is an essential precondition for realizing significant entrepreneurial aspirations that are beyond the personal financial resources of individual entrepreneurs (Bygrave, Hay, Ng and Reynolds 2003, Gompers and Lerner 2004).

The sub-indexes are based on their constituent pillar scores. The pillars, in turn, are based on the interaction between their constituent individual and institutional variables. The incorporation of institutional variables is a unique feature of the GEDI and reflects the qualitative aspect of entrepreneurship. A detailed description of how the different variables are combined to form the 14 pillars and the three sub-indexes is provided in Appendix Tables A.3, A.4, and A.5.

3.2. The Weighting System

What weights should be assigned to the building blocks of the index to account for the components' different influences and their variation across countries? Dynamism is introduced into the index by borrowing a concept from configuration theory, the "penalizing for bottlenecks" (PFB) approach. Configuration theory contends that attributes of entrepreneurship are more meaningful collectively rather than individually (Dess et al. 1993). Thus by "bottlenecks," we mean a shortage or low level of a particular pillar of the sub-index, which when seen in totality can inhibit the overall level of entrepreneurship. The pillars that compose the sub-indexes need to be adjusted to take into account the notion of maintaining the balance between sub-indexes.

The PFB approach works as follows: after normalizing the scores of all the pillars, the value of each pillar of a sub-index in a country is penalized by linking it to the score of the pillar with the weakest performance in that country.

Table 1. U.S. Summary Statistics and Global Index Rankings

Size of population	308.3 million
Per capita GDP (2008)	$46,716
Level of development	Innovation driven
Doing Business Index, 2009-2010: rank/total countries	4/183
Global Competitiveness Index, 2008-09: rank/total countries	2/133
Economic Freedom Index 2009: rank/total countries	6/179
Global Entrepreneurship and Development Index: rank (value)	3 (0.72)
Entrepreneurial attitudes sub-index: rank (value)	6 (0.75)
Entrepreneurial activity sub-index: rank (value)	8 (0.71)
Entrepreneurial aspirations sub-index: rank (value)	1 (0.69)
Weakest pillar to improve (value)	TECH SECTOR (0.46)
Weakest variable to improve (value)	KNOWENT (0.30)

Source: Population—World Bank; per capita GDP—World Bank, purchasing power parity.

This simulates the effect of a bottleneck. The weakest pillar drags down overall performance; if it were improved, the overall sub-index would show a significant improvement. Moreover, the penalty should be higher if differences are higher. Looking from the configuration perspective it implies that stable and efficient sub-index configurations are those that are balanced (have about the same level) in all pillars.

Technically, equation (1) describes the PFB methodology:

$$x_{i,j} = \min y_i(j) + \ln(1 + y_{i,j} - \min y_i(j)) \qquad (1)$$

where $x_{i,j}$ is the modified, after penalty, value of the entrepreneurship feature j of country i

$y_{i,j}$ is the normalized value of the original entrepreneurship feature j of country i

$i = 1, 2,.....m$, (the number of countries)

$j = 1, 2,.....n$ (the number of entrepreneurial features)

Table 2. Global Entrepreneurship and Development Index (GEDI) Rankings

Rank	Country	GEDI Score	Rank	Country	GEDI Score
1	Denmark	0.76	36	Argentina	0.30
2	Canada	0.74	37	Poland	0.29
3	**United States**	**0.72**	38	Croatia	0.28
4	Sweden	0.69	39	Peru	0.28
5	New Zealand	0.68	40	China	0.28
6	Ireland	0.63	41	Colombia	0.28
7	Switzerland	0.63	42	South Africa	0.28
8	Norway	0.62	43	Turkey	0.27
9	Iceland	0.62	44	Mexico	0.27
10	Netherlands	0.62	45	Dominican Republic	0.26
11	Australia	0.60	46	Indonesia	0.26
12	Belgium	0.58	47	Hungary	0.25
13	Finland	0.56	48	Romania	0.25
14	United Kingdom	0.56	49	Macedonia	0.24
15	Singapore	0.56	50	Egypt	0.24
16	Germany	0.54	51	Jordan	0.23
17	Puerto Rico	0.54	52	Panama	0.23
18	France	0.50	53	India	0.23
19	Slovenia	0.49	54	Brazil	0.23
20	Korea	0.49	55	Venezuela	0.22
21	Israel	0.47	56	Thailand	0.22
22	Austria	0.45	57	Russia	0.22
23	Hong Kong	0.45	58	Tunisia	0.22
24	United Arab Emirates	0.42	59	Morocco	0.22
25	Czech Republic	0.42	60	Jamaica	0.21
26	Chile	0.41	61	Algeria	0.19
27	Italy	0.41	62	Serbia	0.18
28	Spain	0.40	63	Kazakhstan	0.18
29	Japan	0.40	64	Bosnia and Herzegovina	0.18
30	Saudi Arabia	0.38	65	Iran	0.17
31	Malaysia	0.36	66	Ecuador	0.17
32	Latvia	0.36	67	Bolivia	0.16
33	Portugal	0.35	68	Syria	0.16
34	Greece	0.32	69	Guatemala	0.15
35	Uruguay	0.30	70	Philippines	0.13
			71	Uganda	0.10

Source: Acs, Z. J., and L. Szerb, "The Global Entrepreneurship Index (GEINDEX)." *Foundations and Trends in Entrepreneurship* 5, no. 5 (2009): 341-435.
Note: Shading indicates countries at the innovation-driven level of development.

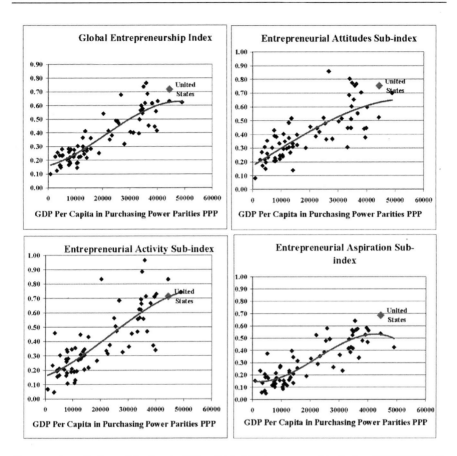

Source: Acs, Z. J., and L. Szerb, "The Global Entrepreneurship Index (GEINDEX)."
Foundations and Trends in Entrepreneurship 5, no. 5 (2009): 341-435.

Figure 3. U.S. Position on GEDI and Sub-Indexes

The bottleneck is achieved for each pillar by adding one plus the natural logarithm of the difference between that pillar's country value and the value for the weakest pillar for that country. Thus, improving the score of the weakest pillar will have a greater effect on the index than improving the score of stronger pillars.

To summarize, the construction of the GEDI begins at the level of the variables, either individual or institutional/environmental. All pillars are calculated from the variables using the interaction variable method, i.e., multiplying the individual variable with the proper institutional variable. The PFB approach is used to calculate the three sub-indexes from the pillars.

Finally, the super-index, the GEDI, is the average of the three subindexes. Figure 2 depicts the structure of the index, giving an overview of how the GEDI is constructed from the variable and pillar levels. The list of participating countries, the years for which data is collected and the sample sizes for each country are presented in Appendix Table 6.

4. THE RELATIVE POSITION OF THE UNITED STATES ON THE GEDI

The GEDI is constructed for a dataset of 71 countries at different stages of development. The United States ranks third overall on the GEDI, just behind Denmark, and Canada, which is a very strong relative position. Table 1 gives the United States's summary statistics on the three major global rankings and on the GEDI.

Table 2 gives the GEDI rankings of all the countries in the dataset. The United States has a score of 0.72 on the GEDI and occupies the third position out of 71. The rankings of all the countries on the three sub-indexes are provided in Appendix B.

Figure 3 displays the ranking of the United States on the GEDI and the sub-indexes. The position of the United States at the top of the curve is evident. The difference is one of degrees and in the composition of countries that are seen to outperform the United States. The drop in position is, however, most clearly evident in the United States's position on the entrepreneurial activity sub-index.

The United States occupies the topmost rank on the entrepreneurial aspiration sub-index. This indicates that overall within the United States, there is still significant effort on the part of early-stage entrepreneurs to introduce new products and services, develop new production processes, penetrate foreign markets, and create high-growth firms. The United States ranks comparatively lower on the entrepreneurial attitudes sub-index with a rank of 6, below New Zealand, Australia, Canada and two of the Nordic countries. However, it does much better than most European countries barring Sweden and Denmark. The United Kingdom ranked number 11 on the attitudes index, and France and Germany, 23 and 24, respectively. The relatively low (8th place) position of the United States on the entrepreneurial activity sub-index is a surprise and a possible cause for concern. It is an indicator that over the last decade the United States may have been lagging behind in terms of opportunity startups and quality of the workforce, as well as its activities within the tech sector. What is even more surprising is a list of the countries that lead. While countries like Denmark and Sweden have consistently performed well, the presence of Ireland and Puerto Rico is somewhat unexpected.

It is possible to track how the sub-indexes and the GEDI have changed over time. In order to do this, we calculate the GEDI and the three sub-indexes' values for the United States for the 2006-2007, 2007-2008, and 2008-2009. The previous publication (Acs and Szerb 2009) was a pooled value for 2006-200 8 so three-year data are not strictly comparable. We also calculate pooled data for 2002-2008 but again the data are not strictly comparable. Nevertheless, they reveal very interesting trends in attitudes, activity, and aspirations.

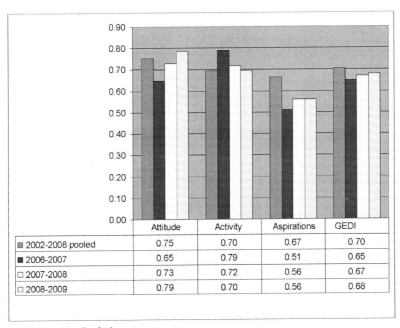

	Attitude	Activity	Aspirations	GEDI
2002-2008 pooled	0.75	0.70	0.67	0.70
2006-2007	0.65	0.79	0.51	0.65
2007-2008	0.73	0.72	0.56	0.67
2008-2009	0.79	0.70	0.56	0.68

Source: Authors' calculation.

Figure 4. Change in the GEDI and Sub-Indexes for the United States, 2002-2009

Figure 4 paints a mixed picture of the United States over the past decade. First of all, the pooled 2002-2008 data shows that the United States did relatively worse on aspirations than on either activity or attitude.

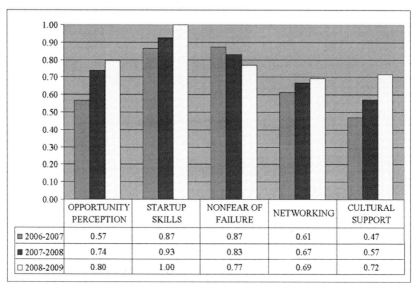

	OPPORTUNITY PERCEPTION	STARTUP SKILLS	NONFEAR OF FAILURE	NETWORKING	CULTURAL SUPPORT
▣ 2006-2007	0.57	0.87	0.87	0.61	0.47
▪ 2007-2008	0.74	0.93	0.83	0.67	0.57
☐ 2008-2009	0.80	1.00	0.77	0.69	0.72

Source: Authors' calculation.

Figure 5. U.S. Entrepreneurial Attitudes Sub-Index Pillar Values, 2006-2009

When looking at the data from 2006 to 2009 we see that while entrepreneurial attitudes steadily increased, entrepreneurial activity steadily declined. On balance the GEDI stayed more or less the same, as the two trends canceled each other out. The entrepreneurial aspiration index increased slightly from 2006-2007 and was steady from 2007 to 2009, but all levels were below the long-run trend.

In order to get a clearer picture of the changes in the sub-indexes over time, Figures 5, 6, and 7 represent changes over the 2006-2009 period in the pillar values of the three subindexes: entrepreneurial attitudes, entrepreneurial activity and entrepreneurial aspirations.

Figure 5 shows that the scores of four of the five pillars of the attitudes sub-index increased, and only one decreased (NONFEAR OF FAILURE). STARTUP SKILLS are improved; both OPPORTUNITY PERCEPTION and CULTURAL SUPPORT show strong increases over time. The cause of the increased fear of failure may be rooted in changing demographics: as the population ages it becomes more risk averse.

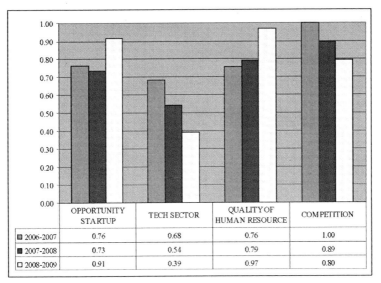

	OPPORTUNITY STARTUP	TECH SECTOR	QUALITY OF HUMAN RESOURCE	COMPETITION
2006-2007	0.76	0.68	0.76	1.00
2007-2008	0.73	0.54	0.79	0.89
2008-2009	0.91	0.39	0.97	0.80

Source: Authors' calculation.

Figure 6. U.S. Entrepreneurial Activity Sub-Index Pillar Values, 2006-2009

The four pillars of the activity sub-index values are evenly split. Two have increased: OPPORTUNITY STARTUPS and QUALITY OF HUMAN RESOURCES; and two have decreased: TECH SECTOR and COMPETITION. The large drop in the tech sector is troubling and is reflected in the pooled data also. The United States seems to have given up something in the sector where it once led the world. COMPETITION also seems to have declined over the decade. This reflects the increasing share of business activity in the hands of large firms and the decline in competition in the economy. This has made it harder for new businesses to get started and for existing ones to prosper. The good news in these trends is that OPPORTUNITY STARTUPS increased in 2008-2009.

The entrepreneurial aspirations sub-index, the one the United States should be focusing on, shows a very mixed picture. Four of the five pillars NEW PRODUCT, NEW TECHNOLOGY, HIGH GROWTH, and INTERNATIONALIZATION have all declined or not changed. The largest increase has been in RISK CAPITAL. An increased pool of financing is a good omen generally, however risk capital does not seem to be translating into new products, new technologies or a greater competitiveness. Not only are the levels of NEW PRODUCT and NEW TECHNOLOGY low, their recent trends are also headed in the wrong direction.

Table 3. U.S. Scores at the Pillar Level and Comparative Standing

Components of Entrepreneurial Attitudes Sub-index (normalized scores)				
	OPPORTUNITY PERCEPTION	STARTUP SKILLS	NONFEAR OF FAILURE	NETWORKING	CULTURAL SUPPORT
United States	0.76	0.95	0.87	0.67	0.60
33rd percentile	0.28	0.34	0.34	0.18	0.28
67th percentile	0.51	0.54	0.69	0.38	0.57

Components of Entrepreneurial Activity Sub-index (normalized scores)			
	OPPORTUNITY STARTUP	TECH SECTOR	QUALITY OF HUMAN RESOURCE	COMPETITION
United States	0.76	0.46	0.84	1.00
33rd percentile	0.23	0.26	0.24	0.27
67th percentile	0.56	0.49	0.49	0.53

Components of Entrepreneurial Aspirations Sub-index (normalized scores)				
	NEW PRODUCT	NEW TECHOLOGY	HIGH GROWTH	INTERNATIONALIZATION	RISK CAPITAL
United States	0.59	0.95	0.56	0.65	0.77
33rd percentile	0.08	0.20	0.24	0.31	0.09
67th percentile	0.31	0.47	0.37	0.62	0.29

Source: Acs, Z. J., and L. Szerb, "The Global Entrepreneurship Index (GEINDEX)." Foundations and Trends in Entrepreneurship 5, no. 5 (2009): 341-435.

Note: Green indicates the U.S. score falls in the top third of the sample (above the 67th percentile); orange indicates it ranks in the middle third (between the 33rd and 67th percentiles).

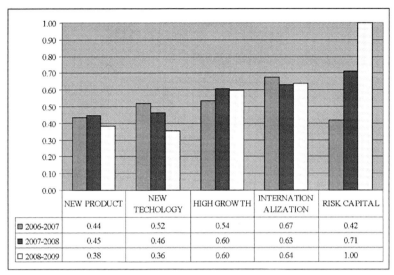

	NEW PRODUCT	NEW TECHOLOGY	HIGH GROWTH	INTERNATIONALIZATION	RISK CAPITAL
2006-2007	0.44	0.52	0.54	0.67	0.42
2007-2008	0.45	0.46	0.60	0.63	0.71
2008-2009	0.38	0.36	0.60	0.64	1.00

Source: Authors' calculation.

Figure 7. U.S. Entrepreneurial Aspirations Sub-Index Pillar Values, 2006-2009

5. RELATIVE POSITION OF THE UNITED STATES AT THE PILLAR LEVEL

The specific strengths and weaknesses of the United States emerge more clearly through the scores on the building blocks (or pillars) of the GEDI. The color coding in Table 3 reflects the U.S. position with respect to averages for all countries taken together. Green indicates that the U.S. value of the pillar is above the 67th percentile value for the sample; orange indicates the value is between the 33rd and 67th percentiles, and red indicates the value is below the 33rd percentile.

Overall, the United States scores well above the 67th percentile level at the pillar level, which is not surprising given that it is among the top 10 in the overall ranking as well as in the sub-indexes. The TECH SECTOR pillar is the only exception.

On the entrepreneurial attitudes sub-index, the United States is comfortably above the 67th percentile level. It scores particularly well on STARTUP SKILLS (0.95) and NONFEAR OF FAILURE (0.87). Where it lags most is on CULTURAL SUPPORT (0.60).

Under the activity sub-index, the United States has a score of 1.00 (the highest possible) on the COMPETITION pillar. Similarly, it scores well on OPPORTUNITY STARTUP and QUALITY OF HUMAN RESOURCES. It is the performance of the United States on the TECH SECTOR variable that is the greatest cause for concern. TECH SECTOR is a combination of entrepreneurial activity in the technology sector and firm-level technology absorption capacity. The area is generally assumed to be one of the core competencies of the U.S. economy. However, it scores a low 0.46 on this pillar, putting it in the middle range, between the 33rd and 67th percentile. The main cause for this is the low U.S. score on the individual-level TECHSECT variable which measures the percentage of entrepreneurial activity that is in the medium- or high-technology sector.

Under the aspirations sub-index, the United States again remains well above the 67th percentile range. It scores the highest on the NEW TECHNOLOGY pillar, recording a score of 0.95. This pillar is a combination of the percentage of entrepreneurial activity where the technology is less than five years old and the degree to which the business environment is conducive to cutting-edge innovations. It thus seems that although there may be comparatively lower activity within the tech sector, a large part of the existing firms are driven by new technology and thrive in an atmosphere conducive to innovation. The United States scores relatively low on the NEW PRODUCT (0.59) and HIGH GROWTH (0.56) pillars.

Figure 8 depicts the strengths and weaknesses of the United States at the pillar level. CULTURAL SUPPORT, TECH SECTOR and HIGH GROWTH emerge as the chief weak points with scores ranging between 0.60 and 0.40, while STARTUP SKILLS, COMPETITION, and NEW TECHNOLOGY are seen to be the strengths with scores close to or equal to 1. It is the tech sector that shows real weakness again.

The spider diagram in Figure 9 illustrates the position of the United States on each of the 14 pillars along with the 33rd and 67th percentile scores for the entire group of countries. Each circle in the graph represents the scores ranging from 0.00 to 1.00. The spider diagram takes the values for each of the 14 pillars and displays the values from 0.00 to 1.00 for each of the pillars. Values that are farthest from the center are largest and those closest to the center are smallest.

This comparison shows not only the weaknesses of other countries, but the strengths as well. In three areas, CULTURAL SUPPORT, TECH SECTOR, and INTERNATIONALIZATION, the United States is only at the 67th percentile, that is, at the average level for efficiency-driven economies.

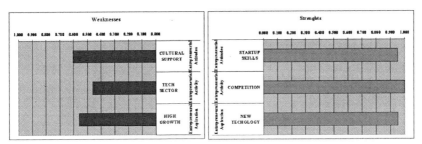

Source: Acs, Z. J., and L. Szerb, "The Global Entrepreneurship Index (GEINDEX)." Foundations and Trends in Entrepreneurship 5, no. 5 (2009): 341-435.

Figure 8. Strengths and Weaknesses at the Pillar Level

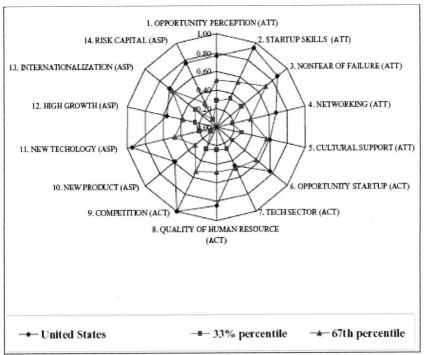

Source: Acs, Z. J., and L. Szerb, "The Global Entrepreneurship Index (GEINDEX)." *Foundations and Trends in Entrepreneurship* 5, no. 5 (2009): 341-435.

Figure 9. U.S. Position on the Pillar Level

Figure 10 compares the United States to India and China. If one looks carefully we see that while the United States has a huge lead in NEW TECHNOLOGY, India is catching up fast; moreover the difference between the United States and China on the TECH SECTOR variable is not very large. The other area of concern is that neither India nor China seems to be afraid of failure. If NONFEAR OF FAILURE indeed captures these countries' attitudes, they are going to present a real entrepreneurial challenge to the United States.

Of course China and India are efficiency-driven countries and are not yet fully in the innovation race. So how does the United States compare to its peers—for instance, the European Union? Figure 11 compares both entities on the 14 pillars. Three observations are important. First, the European Union is as international as the United States. The rest of the world is far behind. Second, the European Union has surpassed the United States in the TECH SECTOR, and the rest of the world is not far behind (i.e., China and other Asian countries). Third, and surprisingly, the CULTURAL SUPPORT variable is at the same level in Europe and the United States.

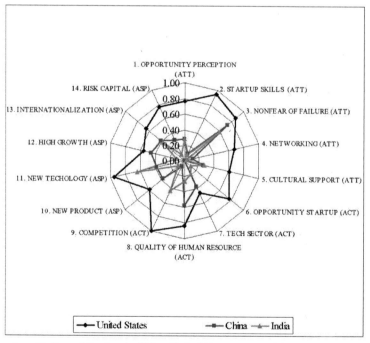

Source: Acs, Z. J., and L. Szerb, "The Global Entrepreneurship Index (GEINDEX)." *Foundations and Trends in Entrepreneurship* 5, no. 5 (2009): 341-435.

Figure 10. Comparison of the United States, China, and India.

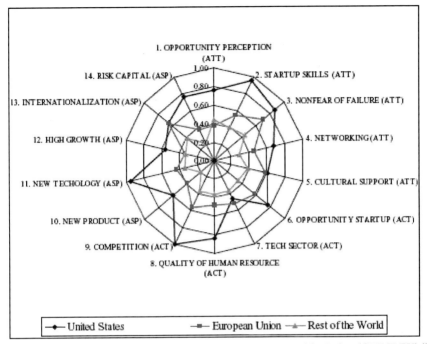

Source: Acs, Z. J., and L. Szerb, "The Global Entrepreneurship Index (GEINDEX)." *Foundations and Trends in Entrepreneurship* 5, no. 5 (2009): 341-435.

Figure 11. Comparison of the European Union, the United States, and the Rest of the World

6. THE U.S. POSITION AT THE VARIABLE LEVEL

Figures 9 and 10 depict the position of the United States at the variable level vis-à-vis the average scores for efficiency-driven and innovation-driven countries in the sample. Under the institutional variables, the United States appears to outperform both the efficiency- and innovation-driven economies by a fair margin on most counts. It does particularly well on the MARKETAGGLOM and VENTCAP variables which give an indication of the size of the market, degree of urbanization, and availability of venture capital. It also does well on the MARK DOM, INNOV, and TECH ABSORP variables, indicating that it is ahead of its competitors in terms of its extent of market dominance, allowing cutting edge innovations, and firm-level technology absorption capability.

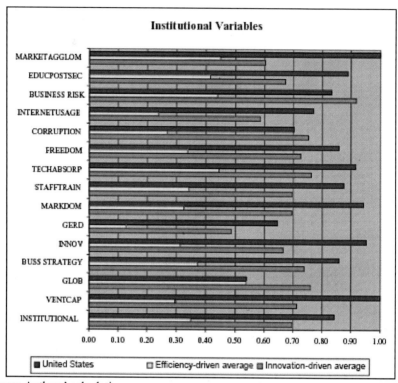

Figure 12. Comparative U.S. Position on the Institutional Variables of the GEDI

The only three areas where the United States appears to lag are GLOB, CORRUPTION, and BUSINESS RISK. GLOB is a part of the Index of Globalization measuring the economic dimension of globalization. The United States appears to be at the level of the efficiency-driven economies on this measure, far behind the average for innovation- driven economies as a whole. CORRUPTION is the perceived level of corruption, as determined by expert assessments and opinion surveys.[11] BUSINESS RISK measures the Country Risk Rate, which refers to the financial, macroeconomic, and business climate. On these two variables, the United States lags somewhat behind the other innovation- driven economies.

Under individual variables, U.S. dominance is relatively weaker. The United States outperforms the country averages on 10 of the 15 variables. It scores particularly well on the NONFEAR, COMPET, and EXPORT variables, maintaining a sizeable gap between its scores and the average scores of the innovation-driven countries. However, its performance on the OPPORTUNITY, KNOWENT, and NEWP variables is below the averages for both the efficiency- and innovation-driven economies. This indicates that the youth's opportunity perception for new business and the population's direct acquaintance with entrepreneurs is more limited in the United States than the country averages. Similarly, it appears that a relatively lower percentage of U.S. businesses bring out products that are new to at least some customers.

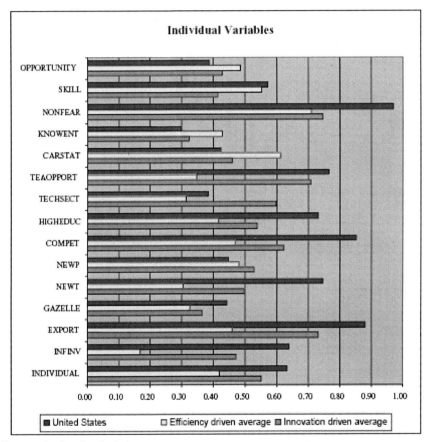

Source: Authors' calculation.

Figure 13. U.S. Position on Individual Variables

The U.S. score lies between the average scores for efficiency- and innovation-driven economies on the TECH SET variable, which measures the amount of entrepreneurial activity in the medium- or high-technology sector.

Table 4. U.S. Scores at Variable and Pillar Levels and Comparative Standing

Institutional Variables		Indvidual Variables		Pillars	
MARKETAGGLOM	1.00	OPPORTUNITY	0.39	OPPORTUNITY PERCEPTION	0.76
EDUCPOSTSEC	0.89	SKILL	0.57	STARTUP SKILLS	0.95
BUSINESS RISK	0.83	NONFEAR	0.97	NONFEAR OF FAILURE	0.87
INTERNETUSAGE	0.77	KNOWENT	0.30	NETWORKING	0.67
CORRUPTION	0.70	CARSTAT	0.42	CULTURAL SUPPORT	0.60
FREEDOM	0.86	TEAOPPORT	0.77	OPPORTUNITY STARTUP	0.76
TECHABSORP	0.92	TECHSECT	0.38	TECH SECTOR	0.46
STAFFTRAIN	0.88	HIGHEDUC	0.73	QUALITY OF HUMAN RESOURCE	0.84
MARKDOM	0.94	COMPET	0.85	COMPETITION	1.00
GERD	0.65	NEWP	0.45	NEW PRODUCT	0.59
INNOV	0.95	NEWT	0.75	NEW TECHOLOGY	0.95
BUSS STRATEGY	0.86	GAZELLE	0.44	HIGH GROWTH	0.56
GLOB	0.54	EXPORT	0.88	INTERNATIONALIZATION	0.65
VENTCAP	1.00	INFINV	0.64	RISK CAPITAL	0.77
AVERAGE of INSTITUTIONAL VARIABLES	0.84	AVERAGE of INDIVIDUAL VARIABLES	0.63	GEDI	0.72

Source: Acs, Z. J., and L. Szerb, "The Global Entrepreneurship Index (GEINDEX)." *Foundations and Trends in Entrepreneurship* 5, no. 5 (2009): 341-435.

Note: Green indicates the U.S. score falls in the top third of the sample (above the 67th percentile); orange indicates it ranks in the middle third; and red indicates the U.S. score falls in the bottom third.

On the CARSTAT variable, the efficiency-driven economies appear to outperform both the United States and the average for innovation-driven economies as a whole. This indicates that, on average, the youth in efficiency-driven economies appear to be relatively more attracted towards entrepreneurship as a career choice than in the United States.

The main areas at the grassroots level that need to be worked on are apparent in the individual and institutional variable scores. Table 4 details these scores and shows which percentile band they fall within. Under the institutional variables, it is the two variables, BUSINESS RISK and GLOB, where the United States lies in the orange zone, i.e. between the 33rd and 67th percentile values for the sample. These were also two of the variables where the United States scored less than the average for all innovation-driven economies. On the remaining variables, the United States lies in the green zone, well above the 67th percentile.

It is in the individual variables that the U.S. scores give greatest cause for concern. Scores for three of the individual variables lie in the red zone, that is, in the bottom third of the 71-country sample. These variables are OPPORTUNITY, KNOWENT, and CARSTAT. This again brings to light the reality that only a small percentage of U.S. youth that sees entrepreneurship opportunities in the area in which they live, they have few opportunities to interact and possibly learn from other entrepreneurs, and only a small portion perceives entrepreneurship to be a good career choice. This may be the main reason for the lower rank of the United States on the entrepreneurial attitudes sub-index.

The variables SKILL, TECHSECT, and NEWP fall in the orange zone. As mentioned earlier, the TECHSET weakness is reflected in the low score on the TECH SECTOR pillar under the activities sub-index. Moreover, the larger picture reveals that despite high scores and being in the top third of the sample on the other variables of the activities subindex, the United States ranks lower than many countries and is not among the top five on this sub-index. The low scores for SKILL and NEWP variables do not show up in the pillar scores because there are counterbalanced by stronger institutional variables.

7. PUBLIC POLICY APPROACHES

Before going into details about the public policy approaches vis-à-vis entrepreneurship we should clarify the policy applicability of the GEDI. While other indexes have focused on entrepreneurship at the innovation-drive stage, the newly created GEDI takes into account entrepreneurship at all stages of development. First, the three entrepreneurial sub-indexes are not of equal importance. The attitude sub-index measures society's basic attitudes toward entrepreneurship through education and social stability. The activity subindex measures what individuals are actually doing to improve the quality of human resources and technological efficiency. The aspiration sub-index measures how much of the entrepreneurial activity is being directed toward innovation, high-impact entrepreneurship, and globalization.

Second, the sequence of these sub-indexes in development is also important. Attitudes are an essential prerequisite for either activity or aspirations. This is in part cultural, as certain societies (e.g., communism and feudalism) outlawed entrepreneurship. Attitude is followed by activity, and after activity, aspirations become important. In some sense, this process is cumulative over time; however it has large overlaps as well. Figure 14 depicts the sub-index that corresponds to each stage of economic development. In a factor- driven (agricultural economy) the focus needs to be on entrepreneurial attitudes in the population. In an efficiency-driven economy (manufacturing) individual entrepreneurs needs to be encouraged to be entrepreneurs and start businesses. In an innovation-driven economy (knowledge-based economy) some people need to create very large and successful businesses.

A third important aspect of development is the roles of institutional and individual variables. While institutional improvement is vital for factor-driven countries to advance to the next level of development, the enhancement of individual characteristics is increasingly critical for innovation-driven economies.

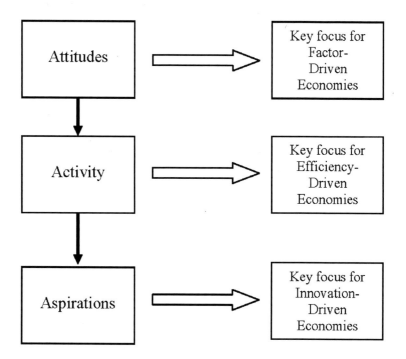

Figure 14. Mapping the Sub-Indexes onto Stages of Development

**Table 5. Policy Emphasis for Economies at
Different Stages of Development**

Stage of Economic Development	Sub-Index		
	Attitudes	**Activity**	**Aspirations**
Factor-driven Economy	**Key Focus**	Develop	Start Enabling
Efficiency-driven Economy	Continuous Improvement	**Key Focus**	Develop
Innovation-driven Economy	Continuous Improvement	Continuous Improvement	**Key Focus**

There are some important policy implications for the countries being at different levels of development, which is summarized in Table 5. Factor-driven economies need to focus on entrepreneurial attitudes, start to develop activity, and begin the process of enabling entrepreneurial aspirations. Efficiency-driven economies' key focus should be on entrepreneurial activity. However, continuous improvement of attitudes and the development of entrepreneurial aspirations are also important. In innovation-driven economies, the key focus should be on aspirations. However, both attitudes and activity need to be improved to maintain balance across the three sub-indexes.

In the following, we are making our policy suggestions to improve entrepreneurship in the United States. In the formulation of the policy steps we considered the improvement of the weakest pillars and the enhancement of the institutional and individual variables of those particular pillars. For the proper policy focus we also took into account the policy suggestions contained in Table 5. Note that these suggestions address the goals of entrepreneurship policy but do not deal with how to achieve these goals.

Area of Concern. According to Table 5, the key focus of U.S. entrepreneurship policy should be aspirations. The improvement of the aspiration sub-index can be achieved by enhancing the weakest pillar, namely high growth. While the institutional component of high growth—business strategy—is rather strong, the individual component, gazelles, is very weak.

Policy Approach: Encourage individuals to start more high-growth firms

Area of Concern. The likelihood of introducing new products is barely higher than the weakest pillar of the aspirations sub-index, high growth. In this case U.S. research and development capability (the institutional variable) is weak but the individual variable (businesses planning to introduce new products) is weaker (Table 4).

Policy Approach: Encourage individuals to introduce products that are new to more people. Research and development should also be encouraged

Area of Concern. Table 5 recommends continuous improvements in activity. The weakest pillar in the activity sub-index is the technology sector. Two decades ago the United States economy was experiencing an explosion in new technology and innovation. The result of this activity was an unparallel prosperity in terms of job creation, productivity and wealth creation. In fact it was one of the most extraordinary times in U.S. history (Jorgenson 2001). We were in this position and the rest of the world just watched. People from all over the world flocked to Silicon Valley to partake in the information and telecommunication revolution. Now, technology sector is the weak spot in U.S. entrepreneurial activity. It is not just that the rest of the world has caught up, the United States seems to have abandoned the sector. The weakest variable contributing to this is the percentage of new businesses in the technology sector.

Policy Approach: Encourage more startups in the tech sectors

Area of Concern: The United States exhibits its greatest weakness in entrepreneurial attitudes. The weakest pillar in the entrepreneurial attitudes sub-index is cultural support for entrepreneurship. The individual variable, career status, drags this down. Individuals do not hold entrepreneurship in high esteem, either as a career choice or in terms of social status. In the institutional variable, the United States scores very well among all countries studied but somewhat lower than Scandinavian and other English-speaking nations. However the main focus should be on the individual variables.

Policy Approach: Focus on improving the image of entrepreneurs and improve the incentive structure to reward productive rather than unproductive activities

Area of Concern: The networking pillar is almost as weak as cultural suppport. The individual variable, knowing an entrepreneur, is much weaker than the institutional variable, Internet usage. In the United States the likelihood of knowing an entrepreneur is no more likely than in a developing country. It is the weakest variable in the index. The other weak variable is the ability to recognize opportunities. The low level of opportunity perception is difficult to identify but it might have to do with the continuing cultural divide in the country.

Policy Approach: Improve entrepreneurial education in secondary schools. Improve public education programs about the value of entrepreneurs to society and the country as a whole

CONCLUSIONS

It is seen that despite the strong performance and leading position in country groupings at the aggregate level, there remain specific areas of concern for the United States. The global perception of the country as a land of opportunity and as the Mecca for individuals wanting to do something new and different seems to be somewhat challenged by the facts. The United States scores relatively lower than Canada and Nordic countries on the entrepreneurial attitudes and activities sub-indexes . It is only in the aspirations index that it maintains the top rank. This seems to suggest that even though the presence of powerful role models and past successes makes Americans have a keen desire to be entrepreneurial, the actual process is finding fewer takers than one would expect. Cultural support for entrepreneurship and the American youth's perception of entrepreneurship as a viable career choice seem to be limited. Firms' performance in terms of growth and employment generation is not as strong, and the tech sector—the beacon of recent U.S. entrepreneurial success—is seen to have a lower score than the sample averages.

There are a multitude of reasons that may explain the apparent slowdown in entrepreneurship in the United States. The crash of the tech sector was certainly a major contributor. With the decline of many of the software companies as the dot-com bubble burst and the economy faced a recession towards the end of the 1990s, there was definitely more caution and a decline in startups. But even more significant are the geopolitical developments that have played out over the last decade that have changed the landscape for business in America.

A direct impact of 9/11 has been felt in the tightening of U.S. immigration policy. Though required due to security concerns and rising domestic opposition to illegal immigration, it has nevertheless affected entrepreneurship in the United States to some extent by controlling the flow of skilled workers into the country. In this respect, countries like Canada, New Zealand, and Australia have all been more pragmatic by giving strong incentives to attract educated, skilled workers to their shores—whether doctors, engineers, or academic researchers—and to keep them there with offers of residency and citizenships. Accompanying a tighter U.S. immigration policy is a growing feeling of disenchantment among large sections of the American population, including the existing immigrant groups, who are at times limited and constrained in terms of opportunities to exploit their potential and skills.

Coupled with internal factors is the reality of what has been going on in the rest of the world. The United States has long been an example for the rest of the world in terms of its capacity for innovation, creation of knowledge, and growth. It continues to outperform Europe overall in terms of its level of entrepreneurship (though the Nordic model may have some lessons for the United States). However, it seems that in many respects a slowdown in U.S. entrepreneurial activities may be a reflection of progress by the rest of the world—learning from the U.S. model and beginning to catch up. Canada, in particular, outperforms the United States in two of the sub-indexes and in the overall rankings.

The findings of this paper should serve more as an eye-opener than as a cause for alarm. The United States maintains its place among the leading entrepreneurial economies. Its performance is still superior in most respects to the averages for innovation-driven and efficiency-driven economies. Its strengths in the skill of its workers, the size of its markets, the institutional support for its people, and the aspirations of the American population are strong and robust. What is required as we come to the end of the first decade of the new millennium is a more pragmatic reality check on some of our perceived strengths and evolving strategies to correct for past shortcomings.

REFERENCES

Acemoglu, D. & Johnson, S. (2005). Unbundling institutions. *Journal of Political Economy, 113(5)*, 949-995.

Acemoglu, D., Johnson, S. & Robinson, J. (2001). The colonial origins of comparative development: An empirical investigation. *American Economic Review, 91(5)*, 1369-1401.

Acs, Z. J., Audretsch, D. B. & Evans, D. S. (1994). *Why Does the Self-Employment Rate Vary Across Countries and Over Time?* Discussion Paper no. 871, Centre for Economic Policy Research.

Acs, Z., Braunerhjelm, P., Audretsch, D. B. & Carlsson, B. (2009). The knowledge spillover theory of entrepreneurship, *Small Business Economics, 32(1)*, 15-30.

Acs, Z. J. & Szerb, L. (2009). The Global Entrepreneurship Index (GEINDEX). *Foundations and Trends in Entrepreneurship, vol. 5(5)*, 341-435.

Acs, Z. J. & Szerb, L. (2011). *The Global Entrepreneurship and Development Index,* Edward Elgar, forthcoming in 2011.

Acs, Z. J. & Varga, A. (2005). Entrepreneurship, agglomeration and technological change. *Small Business Economics, 24(3)*, 323-334.

Ahmad, N . & Hoffman, A. (2007). *A Framework for Addressing and Measuring Entrepreneurship,* OECD Entrepreneurship Indicators Steering Group, Paris.

Audretsch, D. (2002). *Entrepreneurship: A Survey of the Literature.* Report prepared for the European Commission, Enterprise Directorate General. European Commission, Enterprise and Industry.

Audretsch, D. (2006). *The Entrepreneurial Society*, Oxford: Oxford University Press.

Autio, E. (2007). *GEM 2007 High-Growth Entrepreneurship Report,* Global Entrepreneurship Monitor.

Bates, T. (1990). Entrepreneur human capital inputs and small business longevity. *The Review of Economics and Statistics, 72(4)*, 551-559.

Baumol, W. (1990). Entrepreneurship: Productive, unproductive and destructive. *Journal of Political Economy, 98*, 893-921.

Baumol, W., Litan, R. & Schramm, C. (2007). *Good Capitalism, Bad Capitalism, and the Economics of Growth and Prosperity.* New Haven: Yale University Press.

Bhola, R., Verheul, I., Thurik, R. & Grilo, I. (2006). Explaining engagement levels of opportunity and necessity entrepreneurs, *EIM Working Paper*

Series H200610 Zoetermeer, September.

Birch, D. L. & James Medoff, (1994). Gazelles. In *Labor Markets, Employment Policy and Job Creation,* Lewis C. Solmon and Alec R. Levenson, eds. Boulder, Colo. & London: Westview Press, 159-167.

Blanchflower, D. (2000). Self-employment in OECD countries, *Labour Economics, 7(5)*, 471-505.

Blanchflower, D., Oswald, A. & Stutzer, A. (2001). Latent entrepreneurship across nations, *European Economic Review, 45(4-6)*, 680-691.

Block, J. & Wagner, M. (2006). *Necessity and Opportunity Entrepreneurs in Germany: Characteristics and Earnings Differentials,* MPRA Paper no. 610, posted November 7, 2007. Accessed from http://mpra.ub.uni-muenchen.de/610/.

Bosma, N., Jones, K., Autio, E. & Levie, J. (2008). *GEM Executive Report 2007,* Babson College, London Business School, and Global Entrepreneurship Research Consortium.

Bosma, N., Acs, Z. J., Autio, E., Coduras, A. & Levie, J. (2009). GEM Executive Report 2008, Babson College, Universidad del Desarrollo, and Global Entrepreneurship Research Consortium.

Busenitz, L. & Spencer, J. W. (2000). Country institutional profiles: Unlocking entrepreneurial phenomena, *Academy of Management Journal, 43(5)*, 994-1003.

Bygrave, W., Hay, M., Ng, E. & Reynolds, P. (2003). Executive forum: a study of informal investing in 29 nations composing the Global Entrepreneurship Monitor, *Venture Capital, 5(2)*, 101-116.

Caliendo, M., Fossen, F. M. & Kritikos, A. S. (2009). Risk attitudes of nascent entrepreneurs–new evidence from an experimentally validated survey, *Small Business Economics, 32(2)*, 153-167.

Carree, M., van Stel, A., Thurik, R. & Wennekers, S. (2002). Economic development and business ownership: An analysis using data of 23 OECD countries in the period 1976- 1996. *Small Business Economics 19*, 27 1-290.

Davids son, P. (2004). *Researching Entrepreneurship,* New York: Springer.

De Clercq, D., Sapienza, H. J. & Crijns, H. (2005). The internationalization of small and medium firms, *Small Business Economics, 24(4)*, 409-419.

Dess, G.G., Newport, S. & Rasheed, A.A. (1993). Configuration research in strategic management: Key issues and suggestions, *Journal of Management, 19(4)*, 775-796.

Djankov, S., La Porta, R., Lopez–de–Silanes, F. & Shleifer, A. (2002). The regulation of entry, *Quarterly Journal of Economics, 117*, 1–37.

Godin, K., Clemens, J. & Veldhuis, N. (2008). Measuring entrepreneurship conceptual frameworks and empirical indicators, *Studies in Entrepreneurship Markets, 7,* June Fraser Institute.

Gompers, P. & Lerner, J. (2004). *The Venture Capital Cycle,* Cambridge: MIT Press.

Grilo, I. & Thurik, R. A. (2008). Determinants of entrepreneurship in Europe and the U.S., *Industrial and Corporate Change, 17(6),* 1113-1145.

Guiso, L., Sapienza, P. & Zingales, L. (2006). *Does Culture Affect Economic Outcomes?* CEPR Discussion Paper no. 5505. Available at SSRN: http://ssrn.com/abstract=905320.

Hindle, K. (2006). A measurement framework for international entrepreneurship policy research: From impossible index to malleable matrix. *International Journal of Entrepreneurship and Small Business, 3(2),* 139-182.

Iversen, J., Jørgensen, R. & Malchow-Møller, N. (2008). Defining and measuring entrepreneurship. *Foundations and Trends in Entrepreneurship, 4,* no. 1.

Lowrey, Y. L. (2004). *Business Density, Entrepreneurship and Economic Well-Being,* June Available online at *http://ssrn.com/abstract=744804.*

Miller, T. & Holmes, K.R. eds., (2010). *2010 Index of Economic Freedom: The Link Between Entrepreneurial Opportunity and Prosperity,* The Heritage Foundation and The Wall Street Journal, heritage.org/index.

Minniti, M. (2005). Entrepreneurship and network externalities, *Journal of Economic Behavior and Organization, 57(1),* 1-27.

Mueller, S. & Thomas, A. (2001). Culture and entrepreneurial potential: A nine country study of locus of control and innovativeness, *Journal of Business Venturing, 16(1),* 51-75.

OECD (2006). *Understanding Entrepreneurship: Developing Indicators for International Comparisons and Assessments,* STD/C STAT 2006(9). Organization for Economic Cooperation and Development.

OECD (2008). *Measuring Entrepreneurship, A Digest of Indicators,* OECD Statistics Directorate, Eurostat Entrepreneurship Indicators Programme.

OECD (2009). *Measuring Entrepreneurship, A Digest of Indicators,* OECD Statistics Directorate, Eurostat Entrepreneurship Indicators Programme.

Papagiannidis S. & Li, F. (2005). Skills brokerage: A new model for business start-ups in the networked economy, *European Management Journal, 23(4),* 471-482.

Porter, M., Ketels, C. & Delgado, M. (2007). The microeconomic foundations of prosperity: Findings from the Business Competitiveness Index, Chapter

1.2. From *The Global Competitiveness Report, 200 7-2008,* World Economic Forum, Geneva, Switzerland.

Porter, M., Sachs, J. & McArthur, J. (2002). Executive summary: Competitiveness and stages of economic development, In: M., Porter, J., Sachs, P. K., Cornelius, J. McArthur, & K. Schwab, (eds), *The Global Competitiveness Report 2001-2002,* New York: Oxford University Press, 16-25.

Porter, M. & Schwab, K. (2008). *The Global Competitiveness Report 2008-2009,* World Economic Forum, Geneva, Switzerland.

Reynolds, P., Bosma, N., Autio, E., Hunt, S., Bono, N. D., Servais, I., Lopez-Garcia, P. & Chin, N. (2005). Global Entrepreneurship Monitor: Data collection design and implementation 1998-2003. *Small Business Economics, 24,* 205-23 1.

Román, Z. (2006). *Small and Medium-sized Enterprises and Entrepreneurship,* Hungarian Central Statistical Office.

Romer, P. (1990). Endogenous technological change," *Journal of Political Economy, 98,* S71-S102.

Rostow, W. W. (1960). *The Stages of Economic Growth: A Non-communist Manifesto,* Cambridge, U.K.: Cambridge University Press.

Sala-I-Martin, X., Blanke, J., Hanouz, M., Geiger, T., Mia, I. & Paua, F. (2007). The Global Competitiveness Index: Measuring the productive potential of nations, *The Global Competitiveness Report,* 2007-2008, Hampshire: Palgrave Macmillan, 3-40.

Schramm, C. (2006). *The Entrepreneurial Imperative,* New York: Collins.

Schumpeter, J. (1934). *The Theory of Economic Development.* Cambridge, Mass.: Harvard University Press.

Iversen, J., Jørgensen, R. & Malchow-Møller, N. (2008). Defining and measuring entrepreneurship. *Foundations and Trends in Entrepreneurship, 4,* no. 1.

Shane, S. (2009). Why encouraging more people to become entrepreneurs is bad public policy, *Small Business Economics, 33,* 141-149.

Shane, S. & Cable, D. (2003). Network ties, reputation, and the financing of new ventures, *Management Science, 48(3),* 364-381.

Sørensen J. B. & Sorenson, O. (2003), From conception to birth: Opportunity perception and resource mobilization in entrepreneurship, *Advances in Strategic Management, vol. 20,* 71–99.

Terjesen, S. & Szerb, L. (2008). Dice thrown from the beginning? An empirical investigation of determinants of firm-level growth expectations. *Estudios de Economía, 35,* no. 2, 153-178.

Wagner, J. (2002). *The Impact of Risk Aversion, Role Models, and the Regional Milieu on the Transition from Unemployment to Self-Employment: Empirical Evidence for Germany*. IZA Discussion Paper no. 468. Available at SSRN: http://ssrn.com/abstract=310341.

Wennekers, S., van Stel, A., Carree, M. & Thurik, R. (2010). The relationship between entrepreneurship and economic development: Is it U-shaped? *Foundations and Trend sin Entrepreneruship, 6(4)*, 167-237.

APPENDIX A. DATA CONSTRUCTION

Table A.1. Description of Individual Variables Used in the GEDI

Individual Variable	Description
OPPORTUNITY	Percentage of the 18-64 aged population recognizing good conditions to start business next 6 months in area he/she lives
SKILL	Percentage of the 18-64 aged population claiming to posses the required knowledge/skills to start business
NONFEAR	Percentage of the 18-64 aged population stating that the fear of failure would not prevent starting a business
KNOWENT	Percentage of the 18-64 aged population knowing someone who started a business in the past 2 years
NBGOODAV	Percentage of the 18-64 aged population saying that people consider starting business as good career choice
NBSTATAV	Percentage of the 18-64 aged population thinking that people attach high status to successful entrepreneurs
CARSTAT	The status and respect of entrepreneurs calculated as the average of NBGOODAV and NBSTATAV
TEAOPPORT	Percentage of the TEA businesses initiated because of opportunity start-up motive
TECHSECT	Percentage of the TEA businesses that are active in technology sectors (high or medium)
HIGHEDUC	Percentage of the TEA businesses owner/managers with more than a secondary education
COMPET	Percentage of the TEA businesses started in those markets where not many businesses offer the same product
NEWP	Percentage of the TEA businesses offering products that are new to at least some of the customers
NEWT	Percentage of the TEA businesses using new technology that is less than 5 years old average (including 1 year)
GAZELLE	Percentage of the TEA businesses having high job expectation (averaging over 10 employees and 50 percent growth in 5 years)
EXPORT	Percentage of the TEA businesses where at least some customers are outside country (over 1 percent)
INFINVMEAN	The mean amount of 3 year informal investment
BUSANG	Percentage of the 18-64 aged population who provided funds for new business in past 3 years excluding stocks and funds, average
INFINV	The amount of informal investment calculated as INFINVMEAN* BUSANG

Note: TEA = Global Entrepreneurship Monitor's Total Early-phase Entrepreneurial Activity (TEA) index. A TEA business is one of the survey subjects.

Table A.2. Description and Source of Institutional Variables used in the GEDI

Institutional Variable	Description	Source
MARKETDOM	Domestic market size is the sum of gross domestic product plus value of imports of goods and services, minus value of exports of goods and services, normalized on a 1–7 (best) scale data are from the World Economic Forum Competitiveness Index 2008-2009 except 2009 countries that are from 2009-2010.	World Economic Forum, *The Global Competitiveness Report2008-2009*, p. 470. *The Global Competitiveness Report 2009-2010,*p. 450
URBANIZATION	Urbanization is the percentage of the population living in urban areas; data are from the Population Division of the United Nations,	United Nations, http://esa.un.org/unup/index.asp?panel=1
	2005, 2009 countries are from 2010	
MARKET-AGGLOM	The size of the market: A combined measure of the domestic market size and urbanization, which is later used to measure the potential agglomeration effect. Calculated as MARKETDOM*URBANIZATION	Author's calculation
EDUCPOSTSEC	Gross enrollment ratio in post-secondary education, 2008 or latest available data	UNESCO, http://stats.uis.unesco.org/unesco/TableViewer/tableView.aspx?ReportId=167
BUSINESS RISK	The business climate rate "assesses the overall business environment quality in a country... It reflects whether corporate financial information is available and reliable, whether the legal system provides fair and efficient creditor protection, and whether a country's institutional framework is favorable to intercompany transactions." It is a part of the Country Risk Rate. The alphabetical rating is turned to a 7-point Likert scale from 1 ("D" rating) to 7 ("A1" rating). Data are from 2008 except 2009 countries, which are from 2009.	Coface, http://www.trading-safely.com/
INTERNET USAGE	The number Internet users in a particular country per 100 inhabitants, 2008, except 2009 countries, which are from 2009.	International Telecommunication Union, *http://www.itu.int/ITU-D/ict/statistics/*

Institution Variable	Description	Source
CORRUPTION	The Corruption Perceptions Index (CPI) measures the perceived level of public-sector corruption in a country. "The CPI is a "survey of surveys," based on 13 different expert and business surveys." Overall performance is measured on a 10-point Likert scale. Data are from 2008 except 2009 countries, which are from 2009.	Transparency International, http://www.transparency.org/policy_research/surveys_indices/cpi/2009
FREEDOM	Business freedom is a quantitative measure of the ability to start, operate, and close a business that represents the overall burden of regulation, as well as the efficiency of government in the regulatory process. The business freedom score for each country is a number between 0 and 100, with 100 being the freest business environment. The score is based on 10 factors, all weighted equally, using data from the World Bank's *Doing Business* study.	Heritage Foundation, http://www.heritage.org/Index; World Bank's *Doing Business* study, http://www.heritage.org/index/PDF/2009/Index2009_Methodology.pdf
TECHABSORP	Firm level technology absorption capability: "Companies in your country are (1 = not able to absorb new technology, 7 = aggressive in absorbing new technology)." Values for Iran and Syria are estimates since no data exists.Data are from 2007-2008 except 2009 countries that are from 2008-2009.	World Economic Forum, *The Global Competitiveness Report2008-2009,*p. 461; The Global Competitiveness Report 2009-2010 p. 441
STAFFTRAIN	The extent of staff training: "To what extent do companies in your country invest in training and employee development? (1 = hardly at all; 7 = to a great extent)" Iran is estimated as Syria. Data are from 2007-2008 except 2009 countries, which are from 2008-2009.	World Economic Forum, *The Global Competitiveness Report2008-2009,*p. 419; The Global Competitiveness Report 2009-2010 p. 401
MARKDOM	Extent of market dominance: "Corporate activity in your country is (1 = dominated by a few business groups, 7 = spread among many firms)"Iran is estimated as Syria. Data are from 2007-2008 except 2009 countries, which are from 2008-2009	World Economic Forum, *The Global Competitiveness Report2008-2009,*p. 423; *The Global Competitiveness Report 2009-2010 p.* 405
GERD	Gross domestic expenditure on research & development (GERD) as a percentage of GDP, year 2007or latest available data. Values for Puerto Rico, Dominican Republic, and United Arab Emirates are estimated.	UNESCO, http://stats.uis.unesco.org/unesco/TableViewer/tableView.aspx?ReportId=1782

Table A-2 (Continued)

Institutional Varible	Description	Source
INNOV	Innovation index points from Global Competitiveness Index: a complex measure of innovation including investment in research and development by the private sector, the presence of high-quality scientific research institutions, the collaboration in research between universities and industry, and protection of intellectual property.	World Economic Forum, *The Global Competitiveness Report2008-2009*, p. 18; *The Global Competitiveness Report 2009-2010*,p. 20
BUSS STRATEGY	Refers to the ability of companies to pursue distinctive strategies, which involves differentiated positioning and innovative means of production and service delivery. Iran is estimated as Syria. Data are from 2007-2008 except 2009 countries, which are from 2008-2009	World Economic Forum, *The Global Competitiveness Report2008-2009*,p. 18; *The Global Competitiveness Report 2009-2010*, p. 20
GLOB	A part of the Globalization Index measuring the economic dimension of globalization. The variable involves the actual flows of trade, foreign direct investment, portfolio investment, and income payments to foreign nationals, as well as restrictions of hidden import barriers, mean tariff rate, taxes on international trade and capital account restrictions.	KOF Swiss Economic Institute; Axel Dreher (2006): "Does globalization affect growth? Evidence from a new index of globalization," *Appl-ied Economics 38*, 10: 1091-1110. *http:// globalization.kof.ethz.ch/ static/pdf/variables_*.pdf
VENTCAP	A measure of the venture capital availability on a 7-point Likert scale generated from the statement: "Entrepreneurs with innovative but risky projects can generally find venture capital in your country (1 = not true, 7 = true)" Iran is estimated as Syria. Data are from 2007-2008 except 2009 countries, which are from 2008-2009	World Economic Forum, *The Global Competitiveness Report2008-2009*, p. 453; *The Global Competitiveness Report 2009-2010*,p. 433

Table A.3. Description of the Applied Variables and Pillars of the Entrepreneurial Attitude Sub-Index

Individual Variable	Institutional Variable	Calculation	Pillar
OPPORTUNITY is defined as the percentage of the 18-64 population identifying good opportunity in the area they live.	MARKETAGGLOM is defined as the size of the market combined with the level of urbanization on a seven point Likert scale.	OPPORTUNITY x MARKETAGGLOM	OPPORTUNITY PERCEPTION
SKILL is defined as the percentage of the 18-64 population claiming to posses the required knowledge/skills to start business	EDUC is the percentage of the population enrolled in post-secondary education.	SKILL x EDUC	STARTUP SKILLS
NONFEAR is defined as the percentage of the 18-64 aged population stating that the fear of failure would not prevent starting a business	CRR is the Country Risk Rate that refers to the financial, macroeconomic and business climate. The alphabetical rating is turned to a seven point Likert scale to fit to our data set.	NONFEAR x CRR	NONFEAR OF FAILURE
KNOWENT is defined as the percentage of the 18-64 population who knows an entrepreneur personally who started a business in past two years.	INTERNETUSAGE is the Internet users per 100 inhabitants.	KNOWENT x INTERNETUSAGE	NETWORKING
CARSTAT is the average of the percentages of the 18-64 population who say that entrepreneurship is a good carrier choice and has high social status.	CPI is the perceived levels of corruption, as determined by expert assessments and opinion surveys on a seven point Likert scale.	CARSTAT x CPI	CULTURAL SUPPORT

Table A.4. Description of the Applied Variables and Pillars of the Entrepreneurial Activity Sub-Index

Individual Variable	Institutional Variable	Calculation	Pillar
TEAOPPORT is the percentage of the 18-64 population who are nascent entrepreneurs or who own and manage a business aged less than 3.5 years and started the business because of opportunity motivation divided by the TEA	FREEDOM is the freedom of the economy is one sub-index of the overall economic freedom score for each country, where 100 represents the maximum freedom	TEAOPPORT x FREEDOM	OPPORTUNIT YSTARTUP
TECHSECT is the percentages of TEA that are in the medium- or high-tech sector	TECHABSORP indicates firm-level technology absorption capability	TECHSECT x TECHABSORP	TECHNOLOGY SECTOR
HIGHEDUC is the percentage of TEA entrepreneurs having participated at least in post-secondary education.	STAFFTRAIN indicates the extent of staff training	HIGHEDUC x STAFFTRAIN	QUALITY OF HUMAN RESOURCES
COMPET is the percentage of TEA started in those markets where not many businesses offer the same product	MARKDOM indicates the extent of market dominance	COMPET x MARKDOM	COMPETITION

Note: TEA = Global Entrepreneurship Monitor's Total Early-phase Entrepreneurial Activity (TEA) index. A TEA business is one of the survey subjects.

Table A.5. Description of the Applied Variables and Pillars of the Entrepreneurial Activity Sub-Index

Individual Variable	Institutional Variable	Calculation	Pillar
NEWP is the percentage of TEA business where entrepreneurs offer a product that is new to at least some customers	GERD is the R&D percentage of GDP	NEWPROD x GERD	NEW PRODUCT
NEWT is defined as the percentage of TEA business where the technology is less than 5 year old	INNOVCAT is a measure of whether a business environment allows cutting edge innovations	NEWT x INNOVCAT	NEW TECH
GAZELLE is defined as the percentage of high-growth TEA business (employing 10 plus persons and over 50 percent growth in 5 years)	BUSS refers to the ability of companies to pursue distinctive strategies, which involves differentiated positioning and innovative means of production and service delivery	GAZELLE x BUSS	HIGH GROWTH
EXPORT is the percentage of TEA businesses exporting at least 1 percent of product	GLOB is a part of the Index of Globalization measuring the economic dimension of globalization.	EXPORT x GLOB	INTERNATION ALIZATION
INFINV is defined as the percentage of informal investors in the 18-64 aged population multiplied by the average amount of informal investment.	VENTCAP is a measure of the venture capital availability on a 7-point Likert scale	INFINV x VENTCAP	RISK CAPITAL

Note: TEA = Global Entrepreneurship Monitor's Total Early-phase Entrepreneurial Activity (TEA) index. A TEA business is one of the survey subjects.

Table A.6. Countries Included in the GEDI: Size of the Sample by Year

Country	2002	2003	2004	2005	2006	2007	2008	2009	Total
Algeria	-	-	-	-	-	-	-	2,000	2,000
Argentina	1,999	2,004	2,003	2,008	2,007	2,018	2,031	-	14,070
Australia	3,378	2,212	1,991	2,465	2,518	-	-	-	12,564
Austria	-	-	-	2,197	-	2,002	-	-	4,199
Belgium	4,057	2,184	3,879	4,047	2,001	2,028	1,997	-	20,193
Bolivia	-	-	-	-	-	-	2,000	-	2,000
Bosnia and Herzegovina	-	-	-	-	-	-	2,028	-	2,028
Brazil	2,000	2,000	4,000	2,000	2,000	2,000	2,000	-	16,000
Canada	2,007	2,028	2,451	6,418	2,038	-	-	-	14,942
Chile	2,016	1,992	-	1,997	2,007	4,008	4,515	-	16,535
China	2,054	1,607	-	2,109	2,399	2,666	-	-	10,835
Colombia	-	-	-	-	2,001	2,102	2,001	-	6,104
Croatia	2,001	2,000	2,016	2,000	2,000	2,000	1,996	-	14,013
Czech Republic	-	-	-	-	2,001	-	-	-	2,001
Denmark	2,009	2,008	2,009	2,010	10,000	2,001	2,012	-	22,049
Dominican Republic	-	-	-	-	-	2,081	2,019	-	4,100
Ecuador	-	-	2,010	-	-	-	2,142	-	4,152
Egypt	-	-	-	-	-	-	2,636	-	2,636
Finland	2,005	2,005	2,000	2,010	2,005	2,005	2,011	-	14,041
France	2,029	2,018	1,953	2,005	1,909	2,005	2,018	-	13,937
Germany	15,041	7,534	7,523	6,577	4,049	-	4,751	-	45,475
Greece	-	2,000	2,008	2,000	2,000	2,000	2,000	-	12,008
Guatemala	-	-	-	-	-	-	-	2,163	2,163
Hong Kong	2,000	2,000	2,004	-	-	2,058	-	-	8,062
Hungary	2,000	-	2,878	2,878	2,500	1,500	2,001	-	13,757

Country	2002	2003	2004	2005	2006	2007	2008	2009	Total
Iceland	2,000	2,011	2,002	2,002	2,001	2,002	2,002	-	14,020
India	3,047	-	-	-	1,999	1,662	2,032	-	8,740
Indonesia	-	-	-	-	2,000	-	-	-	2,000
Iran	-	-	-	-	-	-	3,124	-	3,124
Ireland	2,000	2,000	1,978	2,000	2,008	2,007	2,001	-	13,994
Israel	2,004	-	1,933	-	-	2,019	2,030	-	7,986
Italy	2,002	2,003	2,945	2,001	1,999	2,000	3,000	-	15,950
Jamaica	-	-	-	2,180	3,669	-	2,407	-	8,256
Japan	1,999	2,000	1,917	2,000	2,000	1,860	2,001	-	13,777
Jordan	-	-	-	-	-	-	-	2,006	2,006
Kazakhstan	-	-	-	-	-	2,000	-	-	2,000
Korea	2,015	-	-	-	-	-	2,000	-	4,015
Latvia	-	-	-	1,964	1,958	2,000	2,011	-	7,933
Macedonia	-	-	-	-	-	-	2,000	-	2,000
Malaysia	-	-	-	-	2,005	-	-	-	2,005
Mexico	1,002	-	-	2,011	2,015	-	2,605	-	7,633
Morocco	-	-	-	-	-	-	-	2,001	2,001
Netherlands	3,510	3,505	3,507	3,582	3,535	3,539	3,508	-	24,686
New Zealand	2,000	2,009	1,933	1,003	-	-	-	-	6,945
Norway	2,036	2,040	2,883	2,015	1,999	2,037	2,049	-	15,059
Panama	-	-	-	-	-	-	-	2,000	2,000
Peru	-	-	2,007	-	1,997	2,000	2,052	-	8,056
Philippines	-	-	-	-	2,000	-	-	-	2,000
Poland	2,000	-	2,001	-	-	-	-	-	4,001
Portugal	-	-	1,000	-	-	2,023	-	-	3,023
Puerto Rico	-	-	-	-	-	1,998	-	-	1,998
Romania	-	-	-	-	-	2,046	2,206	-	4,252
Russia	2,190	-	-	-	1,894	1,939	1,660	-	7,683

Table A-6 (Continued)

Country	2002	2003	2004	20005	2006	2007	2008	2009	Total
Saudi Arabia	-	-	-	-	-	-	-	1,881	1,881
Serbia	-	-	-	-	-	2,200	2,297		4,497
Singapore	2,005	2,008	3,852	4,004	4,011	-	-		15,880
Slovenia	2,030	2,012	2,003	3,016	3,008	3,020	3,019		18,108
South Africa	6,993	3,262	3,252	3,268	3,248	-	3,270		23,293
Spain	2,000	2,000	16,980	19,384	28,306	27,880	30,879		127,429
Sweden	2,000	2,025	26,700	2,002	2,003	2,001	-		36,731
Switzerland	2,001	2,003	-	5,456	-	2,148	-		11,608
Syria	-	-	-	-	-	-	-	2,002	2,002
Thailand	1,043	-	-	2,000	2,000	2,000	-		7,043
Tunisia	-	-	-	-	-	-	-	1,994	1,994
Turkey	-	-	-	-	2,417	2,400	2,400		7,217
Uganda	-	1,035	2,005	-	-	-	-		3,040
United Arab Emirates	-	-	-	-	2,001	2,180	-		4,181
United Kingdom	16,002	22,010	24,006	11,203	43,033	42,713	8,000		166,967
United States	7,059	9,197	14,914	2,021	2,080	2,166	5,249		42,686
Uruguay	-	-	-	-	1,997	2,000	2,027		6,024
Venezuela	-00	2,0	-	2,000	-	1,794	-		5,794
Total	**113,534**	**96,712**	**156,543**	**117,833**	**170,618**	**156,108**	**135,987**	**16,047**	**963,382**

APPENDIX B. COUNTRY RANKINGS

Table B.1. The Global Entrepreneurship Sub-index Country Scores and Ranks

Country	GEDI		Attitude		Activities		Aspirations	
	Score	Rank	Score	Rank	Score	Rank	Score	Rank
Denmark	**0.76**	**1**	**0.75**	**5**	**0.97**	**1**	**0.57**	**6**
Canada	0.74	2	0.77	3	0.89	2	0.55	9
United States	0.72	3	0.75	6	0.71	8	0.69	1
Sweden	0.69	4	0.77	4	0.71	7	0.57	5
New Zealand	0.68	5	0.86	1	0.69	11	0.49	14
Ireland	0.63	6	0.52	14	0.83	4	0.54	10
Switzerland	0.63	7	0.60	12	0.73	6	0.56	8
Norway	0.62	8	0.70	8	0.74	5	0.43	20
Iceland	0.62	9	0.65	10	0.56	18	0.64	2
Netherlands	0.62	10	0.70	7	0.67	12	0.48	16
Australia	0.60	11	0.80	2	0.56	16	0.43	19
Belgium	0.58	12	0.51	18	0.69	10	0.52	13
Finland	0.56	13	0.69	9	0.62	14	0.39	24
United Kingdom	0.56	14	0.60	11	0.66	13	0.42	21
Singapore	0.56	15	0.38	35	0.71	9	0.58	3
Germany	0.54	16	0.45	24	0.62	15	0.56	7
Puerto Rico	0.54	17	0.46	22	0.83	3	0.33	31
France	0.50	18	0.45	23	0.56	19	0.49	15
Slovenia	0.49	19	0.52	15	0.56	17	0.39	25
Korea	0.49	20	0.48	21	0.51	20	0.48	17
Israel	0.47	21	0.37	38	0.47	21	0.58	4
Austria	0.45	22	0.55	13	0.47	22	0.34	30
Hong Kong	0.45	23	0.44	27	0.37	29	0.53	11
United Arab Emirates	0.42	24	0.45	25	0.34	35	0.47	18
Czech Republic	0.42	25	0.39	33	0.34	36	0.53	12
Chile	0.41	26	0.52	16	0.33	37	0.39	23
Italy	0.41	27	0.50	19	0.36	30	0.36	27
Spain	0.40	28	0.52	17	0.45	25	0.24	38
Japan	0.40	29	0.31	47	0.47	23	0.42	22
Saudi Arabia	0.38	30	0.42	29	0.37	28	0.35	28

Table B.1. (Continued)

Country	GEDI		Attitude		Activities		Aspirations	
	Score	Rank	Score	Rank	Score	Rank	Score	Rank
Malaysia	0.36	31	0.49	20	0.45	26	0.16	51
Latvia	0.36	32	0.40	31	0.43	27	0.25	37
Portugal	0.35	33	0.45	26	0.32	40	0.29	33
Greece	0.32	34	0.37	37	0.33	39	0.26	36
Uruguay	0.30	35	0.40	30	0.35	31	0.15	54
Argentina	0.30	36	0.38	36	0.31	41	0.22	41
Poland	0.29	37	0.31	45	0.21	55	0.34	29
Croatia	0.28	38	0.32	44	0.22	52	0.31	32
Peru	0.28	39	0.43	28	0.28	47	0.14	56
China	0.28	40	0.26	54	0.21	53	0.37	26
Colombia	0.28	41	0.38	34	0.28	45	0.17	49
South Africa	0.28	42	0.22	60	0.34	33	0.26	35
Turkey	0.27	43	0.31	46	0.28	46	0.23	39
Mexico	0.27	44	0.33	43	0.34	32	0.13	59
Dominican Republic	0.26	45	0.39	32	0.26	50	0.13	58
Indonesia	0.26	46	0.17	68	0.46	24	0.14	57
Hungary	0.25	47	0.30	49	0.27	49	0.19	44
Romania	0.25	48	0.27	53	0.29	44	0.18	47
Macedonia	0.24	49	0.25	56	0.21	54	0.27	34
Egypt	0.24	50	0.23	58	0.30	43	0.18	48
Jordan	0.23	51	0.35	39	0.16	64	0.18	45
Panama	0.23	52	0.30	50	0.27	48	0.11	65
India	0.23	53	0.22	62	0.23	51	0.23	40
Brazil	0.23	54	0.33	42	0.19	60	0.16	53
Venezuela	0.22	55	0.35	40	0.19	59	0.13	60
Thailand	0.22	56	0.21	66	0.33	38	0.13	61
Russia	0.22	57	0.14	70	0.30	42	0.21	43
Tunisia	0.22	58	0.21	64	0.34	34	0.10	66
Morocco	0.22	59	0.34	41	0.14	67	0.17	50
Jamaica	0.21	60	0.30	48	0.21	56	0.12	64
Algeria	0.19	61	0.23	59	0.18	63	0.16	52
Serbia	0.18	62	0.29	51	0.13	68	0.12	63
Kazakhstan	0.18	63	0.25	55	0.19	61	0.10	67
Bosnia and Herzegovina	0.18	64	0.21	63	0.11	69	0.22	42
Iran	0.17	65	0.24	57	0.18	62	0.09	68

Table B.1. (Continued)

Country	GEDI		Attitude		Activities		Aspirations	
	Score	Rank	Score	Rank	Score	Rank	Score	Rank
Ecuador	0.17	66	0.21	65	0.16	65	0.13	62
Bolivia	0.16	67	0.22	61	0.20	58	0.07	69
Syria	0.16	68	0.15	69	0.16	66	0.18	46
Guatemala	0.15	69	0.20	67	0.20	57	0.05	71
Philippines	0.13	70	0.27	52	0.05	71	0.06	70
Uganda	0.10	71	0.08	71	0.07	70	0.15	55

Table B.2. Entrepreneurial Attitudes Sub-Index and Pillar Scores by Country

Country	Attitudes Sub-Index	Opportunity Perception	Startup Skills	Nonfear of Failure	Networking	Cultural Support
New Zealand	0.86	0.66	1.00	0.92	0.95	0.91
Australia	0.80	0.84	0.81	0.84	0.77	0.76
Canada	0.77	0.76	0.69	0.95	0.64	0.90
Sweden	0.77	0.62	0.74	0.84	0.95	0.76
Denmark	0.75	0.92	0.58	0.81	0.70	0.87
United States	0.75	0.76	0.95	0.87	0.67	0.60
Netherlands	0.70	0.65	0.44	0.97	0.73	1.00
Norway	0.70	0.55	0.67	1.00	0.63	0.77
Finland	0.69	0.48	0.72	0.85	0.66	0.88
Iceland	0.65	0.41	0.64	0.54	1.00	0.92
United Kingdom	0.60	0.76	0.62	0.71	0.36	0.76
Switzerland	0.60	0.42	0.45	0.85	0.63	0.79
Austria	0.55	0.42	0.51	0.75	0.56	0.60
Ireland	0.52	0.34	0.61	0.69	0.35	0.79
Slovenia	0.52	0.16	0.74	0.91	0.76	0.54
Chile	0.52	0.54	0.56	0.71	0.27	0.72
Spain	0.52	0.54	0.63	0.54	0.36	0.58
Belgium	0.51	0.39	0.48	0.93	0.34	0.57
Italy	0.50	0.44	0.52	0.67	0.44	0.44
Malaysia	0.49	0.53	0.29	0.56	0.69	0.48
Korea	0.48	0.15	0.52	0.83	0.85	0.50

Table B.2. (Continued)

Country	Attitudes Sub-Index	Opportunity Perception	Startup Skills	Nonfear of Failure	Networking	Cultural Support
Puerto Rico	0.46	0.44	0.50	0.80	0.23	0.53
France	0.45	0.26	0.34	0.68	0.49	0.62
Germany	0.45	0.26	0.34	0.63	0.43	0.72
United Arab Emirates	0.45	0.53	0.21	0.78	0.32	0.62
Portugal	0.45	0.22	0.66	0.69	0.28	0.58
Hong Kong	0.44	0.57	0.12	0.80	0.38	0.75
Peru	0.43	0.75	0.54	0.36	0.30	0.31
Saudi Arabia	0.42	1.00	0.47	0.24	0.27	0.35
Uruguay	0.40	0.50	0.54	0.32	0.18	0.67
Latvia	0.40	0.24	0.49	0.40	0.54	0.40
Domini-can Republic	0.39	0.46	0.55	0.36	0.32	0.30
Czech Republic	0.39	0.30	0.37	0.72	0.29	0.33
Colombia	0.38	0.85	0.40	0.48	0.12	0.37
Singapore	0.38	0.19	0.21	0.80	0.25	0.68
Argentina	0.38	0.88	0.82	0.17	0.16	0.18
Greece	0.37	0.21	0.94	0.46	0.13	0.39
Israel	0.37	0.37	0.47	0.37	0.22	0.47
Jordan	0.35	0.42	0.51	0.15	0.29	0.57
Venezuela	0.35	0.95	0.74	0.20	0.17	0.09
Morocco	0.34	0.42	0.15	0.53	0.40	0.34
Brazil	0.33	0.82	0.21	0.41	0.14	0.28
Mexico	0.33	0.63	0.23	0.67	0.15	0.17
Croatia	0.32	0.17	0.43	0.43	0.41	0.26
Poland	0.31	0.15	0.41	0.60	0.24	0.28
Turkey	0.31	0.51	0.32	0.33	0.11	0.39
Japan	0.31	0.06	0.11	0.98	0.39	0.34
Jamaica	0.30	0.23	0.26	0.21	0.60	0.28
Hungary	0.30	0.06	0.48	0.66	0.24	0.31
Panama	0.30	0.39	0.65	0.11	0.24	0.24
Serbia	0.29	0.31	0.57	0.21	0.21	0.23
Philippines	0.27	0.65	0.43	0.29	0.04	0.18
Romania	0.27	0.17	0.22	0.45	0.31	0.23
China	0.26	0.28	0.10	0.73	0.11	0.26
Kazakhstan	0.25	0.49	0.47	0.22	0.08	0.13
Macedonia	0.25	0.27	0.38	0.18	0.14	0.30
Iran	0.24	0.40	0.33	0.08	0.38	0.12

Table B.2. (Continued)

Country	Attitudes Sub-Index	Opportunity Perception	Startup Skills	Nonfear of Failure	Networking	Cultural Support
Egypt	0.23	0.22	0.44	0.35	0.06	0.21
Algeria	0.23	0.53	0.25	0.16	0.14	0.13
South Africa	0.22	0.19	0.06	0.67	0.04	0.34
Bolivia	0.22	0.39	0.65	0.04	0.04	0.16
India	0.22	0.28	0.08	0.59	0.03	0.27
Bosnia and Herzego-vina	0.21	0.19	0.37	0.07	0.24	0.25
Tunisia	0.21	0.05	0.24	0.11	0.23	0.52
Ecuador	0.21	0.36	0.40	0.17	0.10	0.09
Thailand	0.21	0.04	0.35	0.39	0.07	0.30
Guatemala	0.20	0.38	0.23	0.13	0.12	0.16
Indonesia	0.17	0.36	0.16	0.31	0.06	0.05
Syria	0.15	0.44	0.15	0.00	0.11	0.15
Russia	0.14	0.20	0.17	0.30	0.10	0.00
Uganda	0.08	0.00	0.00	0.21	0.00	0.25

Table B.3. Entrepreneurial Activity Sub-Index and Pillar Scores by Country

Country	Activities Sub-Index	Opportunity Startup	Technology Sector	Quality of Human Resource	Competition
Denmark	0.97	1.00	0.95	1.00	0.92
Canada	0.89	0.81	1.00	0.90	0.85
Puerto Rico	0.83	0.68	0.82	0.95	0.96
Ireland	0.83	0.77	0.90	0.76	0.93
Norway	0.74	0.78	0.83	0.66	0.73
Switzerland	0.73	0.66	0.84	0.64	0.80
Sweden	0.71	0.89	0.82	0.49	0.82
United States	0.71	0.76	0.46	0.84	1.00
Singapore	0.71	0.87	0.86	0.85	0.46
Belgium	0.69	0.82	0.61	0.75	0.62
New Zealand	0.69	0.91	0.80	0.48	0.69
Netherlands	0.67	0.74	0.76	0.43	0.89
United Kingdom	0.66	0.73	0.54	0.58	0.87

Table B.3. (Continued)

Country	Activities Sub-Index	Opportunity Startup	Technology Sector	Quality of Human Resource	Competition
Finland	0.62	0.76	0.61	0.56	0.59
Germany	0.62	0.58	0.85	0.41	0.80
Australia	0.56	0.75	0.85	0.19	0.91
Slovenia	0.56	0.56	0.69	0.46	0.58
Iceland	0.56	0.82	0.67	0.41	0.43
France	0.56	0.55	0.43	0.63	0.67
Korea	0.51	0.35	0.68	0.80	0.33
Israel	0.47	0.34	0.89	0.58	0.27
Austria	0.47	0.61	0.46	0.21	0.83
Japan	0.47	0.60	0.68	0.40	0.29
Indonesia	0.46	0.24	0.49	0.70	0.57
Spain	0.45	0.57	0.42	0.38	0.47
Malaysia	0.45	0.56	0.38	0.37	0.50
Latvia	0.43	0.50	0.38	0.69	0.27
Saudi Arabia	0.37	0.64	0.04	0.50	0.68
Hong Kong	0.37	0.51	0.32	0.41	0.28
Italy	0.36	0.46	0.36	0.27	0.38
Uruguay	0.35	0.19	0.50	0.28	0.56
Mexico	0.34	0.51	0.27	0.40	0.24
South Africa	0.34	0.25	0.31	0.21	0.70
Tunisia	0.34	0.47	0.23	0.29	0.43
United Arab Emirates	0.34	0.17	0.20	0.81	0.34
Czech Republic	0.34	0.27	0.58	0.17	0.41
Chile	0.33	0.30	0.45	0.13	0.56
Thailand	0.33	0.36	0.13	0.69	0.29
Greece	0.33	0.35	0.29	0.36	0.31
Portugal	0.32	0.65	0.10	0.30	0.36
Argentina	0.31	0.19	0.38	0.33	0.37
Russia	0.30	0.18	0.37	0.57	0.17
Egypt	0.30	0.33	0.43	0.45	0.11
Romania	0.29	0.28	0.14	0.69	0.19
Colombia	0.28	0.23	0.26	0.45	0.21
Turkey	0.28	0.21	0.40	0.39	0.17
Peru	0.28	0.28	0.24	0.28	0.31
Panama	0.27	0.46	0.16	0.24	0.27
Hungary	0.27	0.36	0.30	0.32	0.13
Dominican Republic	0.26	0.25	0.30	0.21	0.28

Table B.3. (Continued)

Country	Activities Sub-Index	Opportunity Startup	Technology Sector	Quality of Human Resource	Competition
India	0.23	0.11	0.19	0.26	0.43
Croatia	0.22	0.10	0.33	0.16	0.33
China	0.21	0.00	0.36	0.58	0.08
Macedonia	0.21	0.09	0.24	0.30	0.25
Poland	0.21	0.13	0.26	0.24	0.21
Jamaica	0.21	0.34	0.11	0.06	0.39
Guatemala	0.20	0.20	0.22	0.00	0.53
Bolivia	0.20	0.23	0.20	0.21	0.16
Venezuela	0.19	0.07	0.56	0.17	0.07
Brazil	0.19	0.02	0.26	0.22	0.33
Kazakhstan	0.19	0.20	0.10	0.53	0.04
Iran	0.18	0.13	0.26	0.22	0.13
Algeria	0.18	0.40	0.02	0.17	0.23
Jordan	0.16	0.21	0.03	0.21	0.25
Ecuador	0.16	0.20	0.28	0.14	0.06
Syria	0.16	0.15	0.03	0.17	0.32
Morocco	0.14	0.46	0.00	0.01	0.19
Serbia	0.13	0.04	0.19	0.13	0.19
Bosnia and Herzegovina	0.11	0.06	0.09	0.10	0.18
Uganda	0.07	0.05	0.01	0.04	0.18
Philippines	0.05	0.02	0.09	0.09	0.00

Table B.4. Entrepreneurial Aspirations Sub-Index and Pillar Scores by Country

Country	Aspirations Sub-Index	New Product	New Tech	High Growth	Internatlon Alization	Risk Capital
United States	0.69	0.59	0.95	0.56	0.65	0.77
Iceland	0.64	0.70	0.49	0.45	0.80	0.95
Israel	0.58	0.95	0.93	0.51	0.80	0.22
Singapore	0.58	0.53	0.58	0.57	0.95	0.42
Denmark	0.57	0.75	0.39	0.47	0.53	0.88
Sweden	0.57	0.75	1.00	0.36	0.46	0.53
Germany	0.56	0.56	0.82	0.47	0.81	0.35
Switzerland	0.56	0.71	0.55	0.34	0.65	0.72
Canada	0.55	0.52	0.55	0.5	0.84	0.43
Ireland	0.54	0.30	0.48	0.43	0.78	0.99

Table B.4. (Continued)

Country	Aspira tions Sub-Index	New Product	New Tech	High Growth	Internatlon Alization	Risk Capital
Czech Republic	0.53	0.47	0.39	0.58	1.00	0.36
Hong Kong	0.53	0.23	0.6	0.65	0.93	0.57
Belgium	0.52	0.43	0.77	0.28	0.86	0.55
France	0.49	0.57	0.52	0.26	0.76	0.55
New Zealand	0.49	0.18	0.81	0.34	0.86	0.69
Korea	0.48	1.00	0.71	0.37	0.55	0.17
Netherlands	0.48	0.32	0.53	0.28	0.63	0.83
United Arab Emirates	0.47	0.09	0.32	0.9	0.66	1.00
Australia	0.43	0.36	0.67	0.25	0.48	0.51
Norway	0.43	0.32	0.58	0.29	0.65	0.37
Japan	0.42	0.90	0.51	0.51	0.34	0.14
United Kingdom	0.42	0.38	0.47	0.46	0.49	0.32
Chile	0.39	0.26	0.45	0.59	0.59	0.22
Finland	0.39	0.86	0.42	0.26	0.46	0.16
Slovenia	0.39	0.46	0.27	0.41	0.71	0.21
China	0.37	0.37	0.38	0.45	0.40	0.29
Italy	0.36	0.28	0.35	0.35	0.62	0.27
Saudi Arabia	0.35	0.05	0.6	1.00	0.34	0.21
Austria	0.34	0.61	0.05	0.32	0.7	0.34
Poland	0.34	0.12	0.84	0.23	0.73	0.13
Puerto Rico	0.33	0.15	0.17	0.99	0.55	0.12
Croatia	0.31	0.12	0.36	0.37	0.70	0.19
Portugal	0.29	0.16	0.28	0.25	0.66	0.21
Macedonia	0.27	0.03	0.19	0.28	0.48	0.64
Greece	0.26	0.10	0.37	0.13	0.42	0.4
South Africa	0.26	0.32	0.25	0.26	0.55	0.08
Latvia	0.25	0.16	0.05	0.50	0.62	0.14
Spain	0.24	0.31	0.18	0.13	0.37	0.24
India	0.23	0.11	0.64	0.11	0.37	0.09
Turkey	0.23	0.30	0.03	0.56	0.36	0.09
Argentina	0.22	0.15	0.38	0.33	0.30	0.04
Bosnia and Herzegovina	0.22	0.00	0.09	0.21	0.51	0.47
Russia	0.21	0.20	0.18	0.6	0.25	0.01
Hungary	0.19	0.12	0.29	0.17	0.50	0.01

Table B.4. (Continued)

Country	Aspira tions Sub- Index	New Product	New Tech	High Growth	Internatlon Alization	Risk Capital
Egypt	0.18	0.02	0.20	0.20	0.27	0.27
Jordan	0.18	0.08	0.42	0.2	0.22	0.07
Romania	0.18	0.08	0.00	0.32	0.69	0.02
Syria	0.18	0.04	0.21	0.41	0.21	0.13
Colombia	0.17	0.04	0.15	0.49	0.26	0.05
Morocco	0.17	0.06	0.32	0.13	0.48	0.00
Algeria	0.16	0.01	0.34	0.17	0.19	0.17
Brazil	0.16	0.08	0.49	0.16	0.16	0.00
Malaysia	0.16	0.17	0.10	0.08	0.40	0.11
Uganda	0.15	0.02	0.71	0.09	0.11	0.00
Uruguay	0.15	0.09	0.07	0.30	0.25	0.10
Indonesia	0.14	0.00	0.31	0.08	0.15	0.21
Peru	0.14	0.05	0.19	0.27	0.23	0.02
Dominican Republic	0.13	0.03	0.04	0.28	0.33	0.06
Ecuador	0.13	0.01	0.33	0.12	0.23	0.01
Mexico	0.13	0.14	0.19	0.08	0.30	0.02
Thailand	0.13	0.07	0.25	0.14	0.16	0.06
Jamaica	0.12	0.00	0.15	0.06	0.40	0.04
Serbia	0.12	0.03	0.11	0.24	0.15	0.12
Panama	0.11	0.03	0.16	0.21	0.16	0.04
Kazakhstan	0.10	0.01	0.03	0.26	0.23	0.02
Tunisia	0.10	0.14	0.16	0.12	0.05	0.06
Iran	0.09	0.07	0.00	0.29	0.01	0.10
Bolivia	0.07	0.05	0.03	0.11	0.14	0.05
Philippines	0.06	0.01	0.16	0.05	0.08	0.00
Guatemala	0.05	0.00	0.26	0.00	0.00	0.02

End Notes

[1] For a review of the literature see: Audretsch 2006; Baumol 1990; Schramm 2006; OECD 2008; Hindle 2006.
[2] See Terjesen and Szerb 2008.
[3] The *self-employment rate* measures the proportion of the adult population who are self-employed and not employees (Blanchflower 2000; Blanchflower et al. 2001). The *business ownership rate* is the proportion of the population at some stage of business ownership, excluding public firms and mutual funds. (Caree et al 2003) *Business density* is defined as the number of firms per 1,000 persons (Lowrey 2004).

[4] The Total Early-stage Entrepreneurial Activity (TEA) index measures the percentage of a country's working-age population who are actively trying to start a new business (nascent entrepreneurs) and those who at least partially own and manage a business less than 3.5 years old (a baby business) (Reynolds et al 2005), (Bosma, et al 2008, 2009).

[5] For more details see Iversen et al. (2008).

[6] Wennekers et al. (1999).

[7] See Shane (2009) for a critique of this.

[8] Understanding Entrepreneurship (OECD 2006); Measuring Entrepreneurship (OECD 2009).

[9] The previous version of the index can be found in Acs and Szerb (2009).

[10] Other indexes yield a U-shape (TEA) or L-shape (business ownership, self employment) relationship. Recent research seems to support the upward trend of self-employment, the "U" shape phenomenon (Wennekers et al. 2010)

[11] As measured by Transparency International's Corruption Perceptions Index. For further information, see appendix Table A.2.

In: Global Entrepreneurship
Editors: S. M. Rice and J. L. Steiner

ISBN: 978-1-61209-556-1
© 2011 Nova Science Publishers, Inc.

Chapter 2

THE IMPACT OF INTERNATIONAL COMPETITION ON SMALL-FIRM EXIT IN U.S. MANUFACTURING

Robert M. Feinberg

This econometric study uses Statistics of U.S. Businesses (SUSB) data to examine the impact of trade on small manufacturers. As global trade increases and currency exchange rates fluctuate, concerns about their impact on small U.S. manufacturers increase. Small manufacturers, by the nature of their scale of operations, are less able to insulate themselves from foreign competition than large manufacturers. Although not without costs, large manufacturers have greater leeway in managing the effects of international competition: they can move production offshore, sign long-term commodity contracts in foreign currencies, or use other tactics to weather global shifts.

OVERALL FINDINGS

Increased international pressures in the form of currency exchange rates lead to increased exit rates among very small manufacturers (those with fewer than 20 employees). Slightly bigger manufacturers (20-499 employees) are less sensitive to changing conditions in the international marketplace. High-tech industries are more insulated from international pressures than low-tech industries are.

Highlights

- At the national level, exit rates among overall small manufacturers showed little fluctuation between 1990 and 2004. They had large variations across firm sizes and industries, however. Exit rates of firms with fewer than 10 employees hovered around 14 percent from 1990 to 2004, around 7 percent for firms with 10-19 employees, and around 5 percent for firms with 20-99 employees and 100- 499 employees. Apparel firms with fewer than 10 employees had the highest exit rate, at 22.3 percent; while the exit rate was lowest for firms in the beverage/tobacco industry with 100-499 employees, at 2.9 percent.
- The determinants of exit generally differed by firm size category between 1990 and 2004, but there were some consistent factors. Mirroring conventional wisdom, growth in the overall economy reduced exit, while increases in labor costs increased firm exits.
- Consumer goods industries had higher rates of exit among small manufacturers.
- In low-tech industries where import penetration is significant, a strong dollar leads to an increased likelihood of exit for small manufacturing firms with fewer than 20 employees.
- For the smallest size class of manufacturers studied (firms with 1-9 employees), the impact of exchange rate effects were greater in the 1 990s than in the 2000s.
- Changes in an industry's import share were not statistically significant for firms with 20-499 employees; it was negative but not consistently statistically significant for firms with 1-19 employees across the two time periods of analysis, the 1 990s and 2000s.
- With the results showing some differences between the decades of the 1990s and 2000s, effects of international competition seem to be changing over time. More disaggregated data would be necessary to evaluate this properly, however.

This chapter was developed under a contract with the Small Business Administration, Office of Advocacy, and contains information and analysis that was reviewed and edited by officials of the Office of Advocacy. However, the final conclusions of the report do not necessarily reflect the views of the Office of Advocacy.

Scope and Methodology

This study determines international competition impacts from 1990 to 2004 on the survival of small manufacturers by industry using econometric models. Firm size categories of 1-9, 10-19, 20-99, and 100-499 employees were evaluated. Establishment exits (or business location exits) by employment size of firm were used as a proxy for firm exits (which includes all business locations). This is very accurate for small size categories (which are largely one-location firms), but breaks down as the firm size increases.[1]

Dependent variables included exchange rates, imports as a share of an industry's goods, research and development intensity by industry, large firm expansions, wage growth (to proxy input cost trends), and a dummy variable on whether the industry sells primarily consumer goods or durable goods. Some dependent variables were lagged one year to indicate causation of exit rates instead of correlation with them. The U.S. Census Bureau's Statistics of U.S. Businesses (SUSB), which is partially funded by the Office of Advocacy, was a primary source. In addition, sources included the New York Federal Reserve Board and the National Science Foundation. SUSB switched industry codes from SIC to NAICS in 1998, forcing an analysis of two separate time periods.

This chapter was peer reviewed consistent with the Office of Advocacy's data quality guidelines. More information on this process can be obtained by contacting the director of economic research at *advocacy* or (202) 205-6533.

I. INTRODUCTION

The important role of new entry in promoting employment and growth in the U.S. economy is by now well established. Less carefully studied is the staying power of new entrepreneurs, in particular the causes of exit by small firms. The previous empirical literature on determinants of exit or firm survival has mostly involved cross-industry studies (with relatively few degrees of freedom available for econometric work and no ability to explore the considerable intertemporal variation in entry within industries) or hazard rates of individual firms. Little research has considered differential determinants of rates of exit of different size categories of small firms.

Acs and Audretsch (1989) explained differential *entry* rates by size but only in one cross section (representing the 1978-80 period). Dunne et al. (1988) looked at panels of firms at 5-year intervals from 1963-1982, and at patterns of differing types of entry and exit, but not differentials by size; furthermore, the focus was on description, rather than on explaining entry or exit. Neither study examines data since the early 1 980s and, for this reason little emphasis was given to the increasingly important role of foreign competition. In particular, it might be expected that small domestic firms may bear the brunt of any displacement of U.S. firms caused by foreign competition, however it is possible that small niche firms may be able to take advantage of foreign sources of supply in competing with larger rivals.

This chapter analyzes both the time-varying and cross-sectional determinants of small firm exit rates in U.S. manufacturing over the 1989-2004 period, especially the reaction of domestic firms to the nature of foreign competition as proxied by industry-specific real exchange rate movements (interacted with import penetration by industry). Exit rates for several size categories of small firms will be explained, and explanatory variables will include lagged industry data and macroeconomic variables.

Data were obtained from the Statistics of U.S. Businesses, available from the U.S. Small Business Administration (in collaboration with the U.S. Census Bureau). Data classification for the period spanned the conversion from Standard Industrial Classification (SIC) system to the North American Industrial Classification System (NAICS) system. Hence data from 1989-1998 were obtained for 140 3-digit SIC manufacturing industries; annual data for 1998-2004 were obtained for 86 4-digit NAICS industries. The study will explain small firm exit rates in several employment size categories—under 10 employees, 10-19 employees, 20-99 employees, and 100-499 employees—using industry data and international and macroeconomic determinants as explanatory variables, with data sources including the Census of Manufactures, Annual Survey of Manufactures, Bureau of Labor Statistics, and National Science Foundation. Employment cost and demand proxies will be included as will variables measuring capital intensity and R&D activity. After discussing the relevant previous academic literature on the topic and descriptive statistics on the key variables of interest, this chapter will present statistical findings and discuss their economic significance.

II. LITERATURE REVIEW AND
THEORETICAL MOTIVATION

While there have been a large number of empirical studies investigating the determinants of entry, far fewer have examined determinants of survival or exit of firms. I discuss just a few of the more recent studies here. In terms of theory, Ghemawat and Nalebuff (1985) derive results showing— somewhat counter-intuitively—that small firms are better able to survive demand downturns than large firms when they have comparable costs; however, where scale economies are important (as may be true in many manufacturing industries) the pattern reverses with small firms the first to exit. Turning to empirical evidence, Khemani and Shapiro (1987) analyze entry and exit equations to examine whether their determinants are symmetric. They find that high market concentration acts as a deterrent to entry, and (surprisingly) that high profit industries experience more exits; the latter effect is explained as high profits attracting more entrants who then displace some incumbents. "In general, both entry and exit are deterred in industries where the minimum efficient plant size and its associated capital requirements are high and where multi-plant firms are prevalent" (p. 25).

Dunne et al. (1988) look at the period 1963-1982, describing and explaining patterns of entry, exit, and growth in U.S. manufacturing. They focus on "the relative importance of different types of entrants, the correlation of entry and exit patterns across industries and over time, and the entrants' post-entry size and exit patterns" (p. 513). They find small, relatively new firms to have the highest exit rates, though survival probabilities seem to depend on how firms originally entered the market—most successful are firms diversifying from other manufacturing industries through new- plant construction. Phillips and Kirchhoff (1989) provide evidence that survival rates of new firms is higher than previously thought, with almost half of all new manufacturing firms surviving at least 6 years; furthermore, they report that survival chances are still higher for those new firms showing growth in the early years.

Audretsch (1994) examined data obtained from the U.S. Small Business Administration on more than 12,000 U.S. manufacturing plants established in 1976; he finds that establishments larger on entry had a lower chance of exit over the next 10 years, as did newly formed independent establishments (relative to newly created affiliates of multiplant firms); innovative activity by new firms had somewhat ambiguous impacts on subsequent exit, though it raised survival probabilities over the long-run. Wagner (1994), in a similar study of German establishments, observes no clear link between start-up size and exit rates; he does, however, find the result noted by Phillips and Kirchhoff (1989) for the United States, namely that surviving firms are more likely to have experienced high rates of growth in their early years. Audretsch and Mahmood (1995) involved a further look into the SBA dataset utilized in Audretsch (1994), with similar findings. They do note that improved macroeconomic conditions (proxied by the unemployment rate) lead to reduced exit rates, though no investigation of the role of international factors (as studied in the current project) is undertaken.

Kleijweg and Lever (1996) study entry and exit in Dutch manufacturing industries during the 1980s, and (of relevance to the current project) they find that R&D-intensive industries experience reduced rates of exit. The paper which comes closest to the focus of the current study is that by DeBacker and Sleuwagen (2003). They analyze data on Belgian manufacturing industries to determine the impact of foreign competition (both through imports and inbound foreign direct investment) on entry and exit rates of domestic entrepreneurs. While they find that this international competition does increase domestic exit rates, their results suggest that firms may undertake strategies to respond to foreign direct investment which lessen the impact of competition.

As seen above, little work has examined international effects on survival and exit rates, the focus of this study. Much of my past research has investigated the impact of foreign competition on domestic firms (though I have not previously examined the exit decision). For example, Feinberg (1 989a) found the passthrough of exchange rate movements into domestic U.S. prices to be quite incomplete and to vary by industry factors. Feinberg (1989b) used a simple simulation model to consider the role that an unexpected surge in imports would have on the nature of competition in a domestic industry. Feinberg (2007) identified a pro-competitive effect of foreign competition on pricing behavior by U.S. firms.

Based on the literature above, it seems reasonable to expect that international pressures will affect domestic firm survival or exit rates, and that small firms may be particularly at risk. Demand growth (and perceptions of future growth) should also impact firm exit behavior. As noted above, some authors have found the nature of technology in the industry to affect survival; therefore R&D intensity in the industry as well as its interaction with international pressures, will also be included as explanatory variables.

In explaining small firm exit rates by industry, two caveats must be kept in mind. The first is that the level of aggregation employed here (3-digit SIC or

4-digit NAICS categories) may be too great to capture motivations of heterogeneous firms—i.e, small businesses in niche categories of broader industry groupings may be little affected by aggregate conditions. Perhaps more importantly, the work of Headd (2003) reminds us that business closure (exit) may not always reflect failure; he found that about a third of closed businesses regarded themselves as successful at closure. This suggests that to fully explain the exit decision by small firms, one would ideally like to go beyond the industry, macroeconomic, and international influences considered in this chapter—and consider more idiosyncratic individual explanations for why firms choose to shut down. At the level of industry detail this is not possible, but we should not be surprised if expected patterns explaining small firm *failure* do not seem to well predict *closure*.

III. DESCRIPTIVE STATISTICS

The SUSB data on exit by industry actually provide information on establishment exits. While this can be a firm exit, it also may mean a plant closing by a firm that remains in operation. While the distinction is not made at the level of industry detail used in this study, a look at the more aggregate data for all manufacturing is illuminating. Table 1 presents establishment exits in manufacturing in the four size categories studied here and the extent to which these represent firm exit (for the 2003- 2004 period).

Table 1. Firm Exits and Establishment Exits, All Manufacturing, 2003-2004

	Firm Size (number of employees)			
	1-9	0-19	20-99	100-499
Firm Exits	18,735	2,541	2,439	348
Establishment Exits	18,780	2,546	2,858	1,166
Percentage Firm Exits	99.8%	98.3%	85.3%	29.8%

Source: Statistics of U.S. Businesses (SUSB). U.S. Department of Commerce, Bureau of the Census, partially funded by the Office of Advocacy, U.S. Small Business Administration.

Table 2. Mean Values of Exit Measures by Year
(Percent of all exits in size class)

| | | Firm Size (number of employees) | | |
	1-9	10-19	20-99	100-499
1990	14.6	7.1	5.5	5.1
1991	15.9	7.0	5.4	5.5
1992	15.1	6.8	5.7	4.7
1993	13.7	7.5	5.8	5.2
1994	13.7	5.8	5.6	6.1
1995	14.4	5.6	3.6	4.4
1996	13.6	6.3	5.4	4.9
1997	14.2	7.9	5.3	4.4
1998	14.2	6.8	5.0	5.3
1999	14.3	6.7	5.0	5.0
2000	14.2	6.5	5.0	4.9
2001	14.3	6.6	5.3	4.4
2002	15.7	6.8	5.7	6.7
2003	13.9	6.6	5.2	5.8
2004	13.3	6.0	5.0	5.0

Source: Statistics of U.S. Businesses (SUSB). U.S. Department of Commerce, Bureau of the Census, partially funded by the Office of Advocacy, U.S. Small Business Administration.

Table 3. Mean Values of Exit Measures by Industry Sector
(Percent of all exits in size class)

| | Firm Size (number of employees) | | | |
	1-9	10-19	20-99	10-499
SIC-basis. 1990-1998				
Food and Beverage	13.61	6.61	4.75	4.33
Tobacco	20.57	8.97	7.94	8.70
Textile	15.58	8.88	6.43	4.82
Apparel	20.57	12.57	9.31	8.45
Lumber	15.47	6.78	5.24	5.14
Furniture	15.46	7.92	6.11	5.69
Paper	14.97	9.81	6.22	3.52
SIC-basis. 1990-1998				
Printing	13.34	5.65	4.58	4.76

Table 3. (Continued)

	1-9	10-19	20-99	10-499
			Firm Size (number of employees)	
Chemicals	12.08	5.07	4.12	4.92
Petroleum Refining	13.80	7.76	5.54	4.47
Rubber and Plastics	12.13	6.01	4.82	4.66
Leather	15.85	8.24	6.21	6.25
Mineral Products	13.14	5.26	4.50	4.02
Primary Metals	13.08	5.73	4.16	3.69
Fabricated Metals	12.04	4.88	3.63	4.43
Machinery and Computers	12.32	4.75	3.71	4.73
Electronics and Electrical	14.00	5.57	4.63	4.87
Transportation Equipment	15.32	6.31	5.64	5.43
Measurement and Control Devices	13.10	5.29	4.74	6.09
Miscellaneous Manufacturing	13.63	5.46	4.74	4.46
NAICS-basis. 1999-2004				
Food	13.84	6.34	5.03	4.70
Beverage and Tobacco	17.31	7.97	9.77	2.88
Textiles	15.19	7.90	5.96	6.77
Apparel	22.33	15.72	11.53	9.16
Leather	15.65	8.82	7.76	8.03
Wood products	14.30	6.22	3.98	4.28
Paper	16.05	8.82	4.86	6.32
Printing	11.52	4.92	4.50	5.71
Chemicals	11.38	5.54	4.79	3.71
Petroleum and Coal Products	13.07	5.55	4.72	4.40
Rubber and Plastics	12.97	5.36	4.45	4.44
Furniture	13.58	5.98	4.41	4.41
Mineral Products	14.99	6.54	4.81	4.95
Primary Metals	11.73	4.41	3.42	4.08
Fabricated Metals	12.46	4.87	3.85	4.97
Machinery	16.26	7.79	6.76	7.26
Computer and Electronics	14.21	5.91	4.42	5.41
Transportation Equipment	16.13	6.58	5.21	5.86
Electrical Equipment, Components	12.69	5.77	4.90	4.62
Miscellaneous Manufacturing	11.64	4.43	4.14	5.02

Source: Statistics of U.S. Businesses (SUSB). U.S. Department of Commerce, Bureau
of the Census, partially funded by the Office of Advocacy, U.S. Small Business
Administration.

Clearly, the exit of establishments in firms of under 20 employees can be
safely assumed to represent firm exit. The overwhelming bulk of such exits in

firms of 20-99 employees can also be seen as exit. However, for firms in the 100-499 employee range, establishment exits are more likely to represent firm restructuring or capacity reduction. While this study will examine determinants of establishment exit in this size range, it would not be surprising to find differences among firms as compared to the smaller size ranges in which firm exit is more accurately measured.

We now turn to measures of exit over time and by industry sector for the four size categories considered here. In Table 2 we see relatively little variation in exit rates over the 15-year time frame: 13.3-15.9 percent for the smallest firm size; 5.6-7.9 percent for 10-19 employee firms; 3.6- 5.8 percent for the 20-99 employee firms; and 4.4-6.7 percent for the 100-499 employee firms.[2]

There does seem to be somewhat greater variation across industry sectors, however (Table 3). Exit rates for 1-9 employee firms vary from as low as 11.4 percent (chemicals, in the 1999-2004 period) to 22.3 percent (apparel, also during 1999-2004). For 10-19 employee firms, exit rates vary from 4.4 percent (primary metals, 1999-2004) to 15.7 percent (apparel, 1999-2004); for 20-99 employee firms, exit rates vary from 3.4 percent (again, primary metals, 1999-2004) to 11.5 percent (again, apparel, 1999-2004). For the largest size category considered here, exit rates vary from 2.9 percent (beverage/tobacco, 1999-2004) to 9.2 percent (again, apparel, 1999-2004). Apparel also is the sector with the highest rate of exit in the 1990-1998 period. Clearly there is much cross-industry variation in exit rates to explain in the statistical analysis.

Tables 4 and 5 present descriptive statistics for the variables to be used in the statistical analysis to follow, looking at the full SIC and NAICS samples. Over all industries and years, average exit rates are quite similar in the two samples, about 14 percent for 1-9 employee firms, 7 percent for 10-19 employee firms, and 5 percent for both 20-99 and 100-499 employee firms, confirming the commonly held belief that larger firms are less likely to fail. Also similar is the rate of growth in new establishments by large (over 500 employee) firms, about 3 percent in both samples; this variable is taken to be a proxy for the perceived growth in industry demand (from the perspective of the smaller firms analyzed in this study).

Table 4. Descriptive Statistics for SIC-based Study, 1990-1998

Variable	Observations	Mean	Standard Deviation	Minimum	Maximum
Exit Rate (<10)	1257	14.37	6.39	0	100
Exit Rate (10-19)	1245	6.74	6.67	0	100
Exit Rate (20-99)	1260	5.26	5.14	0	100
Exit Rate (100-499)	1244	5.08	5.34	0	100
Large Firm Expansion	1251	3.36	3.62	0	60
Broad Sector Import Share	1251	16.98	14.93	1.16	56.97
M-Wt Real XR Change	1251	1.85	4.82	-9.76	18.4
R&D Intensity	1260	1.78	2.17	0.06	5.86
Capital Intensity	1260	0.17	0.17	0.01	1.37
Consumer Good	1260	0.37	0.48	0	1
Durable Good	1260	0.26	0.44	0	1

Variable Definitions:

Exit Rate (by Size) = establishment deaths in size category as percentage of previous year establishments by category (Source: U.S. Small Business Administration)

Large Firm Expansion = establishment births in firms over 500 employees as percentage of previous year establishments of that size (Source: U.S. Small Business Administration)

Broad Sector Import Share = value of imports as percentage of "apparent domestic consumption" (domestic shipments + imports—exports), for 1992 at 2-digit SIC level (Source: U.S. Department of Commerce, Bureau of the Census)

M-Wt Real XR Change = annual percentage change in import-weighted real exchange rate index (varying by 2-digit SIC, 1st quarter to 1st quarter changes) (Source: New York Federal Reserve Board, Database on Industry-Specific Exchange Rates, *http://www.ny.frb.org/research/economists/goldberg/papers.html*)

R&D Intensity = total company funds for R&D as percentage of value of shipments, for 1992, at broader 2-digit SIC level (Source: National Science Foundation, Annual Survey of Manufactures)

Capital Intensity = total capital expenditures per dollar of labor costs at the 3 digit SIC level, for 1992 (Source: Annual Survey of Manufactures)

Consumer Good, Durable Good—classifications based on Ornstein (1977), modified as necessary by author.

The main explanatory variables include the following:

(1) a real exchange rate index defined at the broader 2-digit SIC level (normalized at 100 for 1990) for the earlier time period and at the broader 3-digit NAICS level (normalized at 100 for 2000) for the later period. This variable is interacted both with import penetration for that broader industry sector to capture the industry's vulnerability to international pressures, as well as with industry R&D intensity to see whether small firms in knowledge intensive industries can better survive in the face of foreign competition.

(2) real GDP growth; this is included in lieu of industry level growth, which may be endogenous with respect to company behavior.

(3) growth in aggregate labor compensation; this is included to account for effects on exit rates due to cost trends.

(4) growth rates in the number of establishments in firms over 500 employees; this variable can be interpreted as a proxy for growth potential perceived by smaller firms (though it may also reflect the extent to which small firms feel threatened by large firm expansion).

(5) cross-industry measures of import penetration and capital intensity (capital-labor ratios); these variables will proxy the role of barriers to *successful* entry which make failure of small firms more likely.

(6) the (log of the) number of establishments in a particular size category within an industry in a given year (to control for large variations in exit rates caused by one or a small number of exits in an industry/size category cell with only few firms).

(7) product characteristics—whether the industry sells primarily *consumer* goods, *durable* goods, or both.

Reflecting the steady growth in import penetration in U.S. manufacturing in recent years, we find the import share averaging 17 percent for 1992 and a little over 18 percent for 1998. While the sample averages suggest a decline over time in R&D intensity and an increase in capital intensity, this may simply be due to changes in industry definitions rather than any real economy-wide changes. (The NAICS definitions are broader—with 86 industries at the 4-digit level—than the SIC definitions, for which there are 140 industries at the roughly comparable 3-digit level.)

Table 5. Descriptive Statistics for NAICS-based Study, 1999-2004

Variable	Observations	Mean	Standard Deviation	Minimum	Maximum
Exit Rate (<10)	516	14.29	3.81	6.45	38.46
Exit Rate (10-19)	516	6.53	3.43	0	21.43
Exit Rate (20-99)	516	5.2	2.85	0	33.33
Exit Rate (100-499)	516	5.31	3.07	0	23.08
Large Firm Expansion	430	3.44	2.42	0	24.32
Broad Sector Import Share	516	18.21	14.28	3.47	67.48
M-Wt Real XR Change	516	3.19	5.46	-11.81	18.37
R&D Intensity	516	1.05	0.87	0.06	3.71
Capital Intensity	516	0.21	0.13	0.05	0.7
Consumer Good	516	0.36	0.48	0	1
Durable Good	516	0.33	0.47	0	1

Variable Definitions:

Exit Rate (by Size) = establishment deaths in size category as percentage of previous year establishments by category (Source: U.S. Small Business Administration)

Large Firm Expansion = establishment births in firms over 500 employees as percentage of previous year establishments of that size (Source: U.S. Small Business Administration)

Broad Sector Import Share = value of imports as percentage of "apparent domestic consumption" (domestic shipments + imports—exports), for 1998 at 3-digit NAICS level (Source: U.S. Department of Commerce, Bureau of the Census)

M-Wt Real XR Change = annual percentage change in import-weighted real exchange rate index (varying by 3-digit NAICS, 1st quarter to 1st quarter changes) (Source: New York Federal Reserve Board, Database on Industry-Specific Exchange Rates, *http://www.ny.frb.org/research/economists/goldberg/papers.html)*

R&D Intensity = total company funds for R&D as percentage of value of shipments, for 1998, at broader 3-digit NAICS level (Source: National Science Foundation, Annual Survey of Manufactures)

Capital Intensity = total capital expenditures per dollar of labor costs at the 4-digit NAICS level, for 1998 (Source: Annual Survey of Manufactures)

Consumer Good, Durable Good—classifications based on Ornstein (1977), modified as necessary by author.

IV. STATISTICAL RESULTS

Given problems of comparability between SIC and NAICS codes, two separate statistical studies (pooled cross-section time series regression analyses) will be conducted to explain exit rates by firms in the 1-9, 10-19, 20-99, and 100-499 employee size categories, however with the same model specification. Using SIC industries for 1989-1998 will yield more than 1,100 observations, while the use of NAICS industries for 1998-2004 will allow estimation on more than 400 observations.

Timing issues are of course important to consider. The SUSB exit data are for the year ending in March, while the demand and cost proxies, real GDP and the employment cost index, are changes in annual averages—therefore these will be lagged one year. Similarly, exchange rate changes are first-quarter annual changes; as exit decisions should be based on current and expected future competitive pressures, we examine contemporaneous exchange rate impacts on exit rates.

As industries are likely to differ in the variability of exit rates, statistical techniques need to account for this problem. Therefore, estimates will be obtained via feasible generalized least squares controlling for heteroscedasticity (using the *xtgls* command in STATA), with random industry effects.[3]

The basic model is:

Exit$_{it}$ (separately by employment size category) = f(lagged growth in real GDP, lagged growth in large firms within industry, capital intensity, import penetration, lagged aggregate employment cost changes, real exchange rate index value [interacted with both import shares and R&D intensity], consumer/durable goods dummies, number of category establishments, random industry effects)

To start, Table 6 presents results explaining exit rates within the four small-firm size categories in most of the 140 SIC industries during the 1990s. To better judge the role of demand and cost pressures, these effects are held constant across industries (and so the estimated coefficients for these variables may be regarded as rough average effects of these macroeconomic factors). Several results stand out and are remarkably consistent across all four size categories of small firm exit (especially the under-100 employee categories in which *establishment* exit most likely corresponds to *firm* exit):

(1) aggregate demand growth in the economy reduces exit, while cost pressures increase exit rates;

(2) consumer goods industries have consistently higher rates of exit;

(3) for the 10-19 and 20-99 employee categories, capital intensity seems to make exit more likely, perhaps by increasing the amount of financing required not just to enter but to continue operations;

(4) a stronger dollar makes very small firm exit (19 or fewer employees) *more likely in industries where import penetration is significant.* This strong effect is moderated in R&D- intensive industries, the latter result suggestive of high-tech niches that can allow small firms to thrive despite exchange rate pressure (and perhaps these niche categories may rely on lower-cost imported components as the dollar strengthens).

In addition, the number of establishments in each size/industry category is a useful control for exit rates, with smaller groups implying higher exit rates *ceteris paribus.* Other effects are more spotty: larger import shares (independent of the role of exchange rates) seem, surprisingly, to reduce exit rates, but only with a statistically significant impact in the 10-19 employee size category; and durable goods industries have a higher exit rate for the under-100 employee size categories, though not statistically significant for all of these. The previous year's growth rate in large firm establishments (over 500 employees) seems to imply higher rates of exit but the magnitude of this impact is quite small (and only statistically significant for the very largest and very smallest firms in the sample).

Table 7 examines the same issues for the first part of the current decade, using the NAICS-based sample. As noted earlier, the rate of exit rose in all four size classes in 2002, and substantially in the 1-9 and 100-499 employeee size classes. This may have been a response to the uncertainties created in the aftermath of 9/11. To account for this, a dummy variable for 2002 is included in the regression equations (a dummy for 2001 was not statistically significant). This variable has the predicted positive impact for all size classes, both statistically significant and of substantial magnitude for all but the 20-99 employee size category, with exit rates in 2002 between 0.3 and 1.6 percentage points higher *ceteris paribus* (the latter, for example, representing about 10 percent of the mean 2002 rate of exit in the 1-9 employee category).

More so than in the earlier period, the determinants of exit seem to vary considerably by size category. Only for the largest size category does establishment exit respond as expected to economy-wide demand growth (though to the extent that large-firm expansion is viewed as a proxy for expected industry-specific demand growth, we see a significant effect for the 20-99 employee size category as well). Capital intensity no longer has any statistically significant effect on small firm exit. However, of particular interest for this study, international pressures—through exchange rate movements—continue to lead to greater exit (when accompanied by high import shares) for both of the under-20 employee firm size categories. For all size categories, R&D intensity reduces the sensitivity of exit rates to dollar appreciation (statistically significant for all but the largest— 100-499 employee—grouping).

Table 6. Feasible Generalized Least Squares Results Explaining Small-Firm Exit Rates by Firm Size, Heteroscedasticity Across Industries, Random Industry Effects – SIC-based study, 1990-1998

	Firm Size (number of employees)			
	1-9	10-19	20-99	100-499
GDP growth	-0.16***	-0.12***	-0.17***	-0.10**
	(0.05)	(0.04)	(0.04)	(0.05)
Aggregate wage growth	0.73***	0.60***	0.28***	0.32**
	(0.14)	(0.11)	(0.10)	(0.14)
ln(No. of establishments)	-0.48***	-0.25***	-0.26***	-0.15**
	(0.05)	(0.05)	(0.04)	(0.07)
Import share	-0.06	-0.14***	-0.02	0.06
	(0.05)	(0.04)	(0.04)	(0.05)
Mshr*RXR	0.0011**	0.0017***	0.0003	-0.0005
	(0.0005)	(0.0004)	(0.0004)	(0.0005)
Large Firm Expansion	0.05*	0.02	0.02	0.07**
	(0.02)	(0.02)	(0.02)	(0.03)
R&D intensity*RXR	-0.0036***	-0.0037***	-0.0019***	0.0008**
	(0.0004)	(0.0003)	(0.0003)	(0.0003)
Capital intensity	-0.04	2.17***	1.59***	-0.69
	(0.90)	(0.67)	(0.58)	(0.67)
Consumer good	1.78***	0.88***	0.92***	0.57***
	(0.15)	(0.14)	(0.11)	(0.14)
Durable good	0.45**	0.11	0.26*	-0.45**
	(0.20)	(0.17)	(0.13)	(0.20)
N	1104	1079	1104	1103
Wald Chi-squared	617.9***	525.5***	350.6***	65.2***

Note: standard errors in parentheses below estimated coefficients.
*Significant at 10% **Significant at 5% ***Significant at 1%

Table 7. Feasible Generalized Least Squares Results Explaining Small Firm Exit Rates by Firm Size, Allowing for Heteroscedasticity Across Industries – NAICSbased study, 2000-2004 (86 industries x 5 years)

| | Firm Size (number of employees) | | | |
	1-9	10-19	20-99	100-499
GDP growth	0.15*	0.07	-0.07	-0.27***
	(0.09)	(0.08)	(0.07)	(0.10)
Aggregate wage growth	0.14	-0.07	0.29*	-0.55**
	(0.22)	(0.20)	(0.17)	(0.28)
ln(No. of establishments)	-0.67***	-0.27***	-0.13*	0.19*
	(0.10)	(0.10)	(0.08)	(0.11)
Import share	-0.24**	-0.09	0.01	-0.04
	(0.12)	(0.11)	(0.08)	(0.13)
Mshr*RXR	0.0033***	0.0017*	0.0005	0.0011
	(0.0012)	(0.0016)	(0.0008)	(0.0013)
Large Firm Expansion	0.08**	0.01	-0.07***	0.07*
	(0.03)	(0.03)	(0.03)	(0.04)
R&D intensity*RXR	-0.0116***	-0.0097***	-0.0048***	-0.0002
	(0.0016)	(0.013)	(0.0010)	(0.0013)
Capital intensity	-1.07	-0.39	0.73	-0.86
	(1.24)	(1.04)	(0.68)	(0.71)
Consumer good	0.34	0.69***	0.88***	0.45**
	(0.24)	(0.22)	(0.15)	(0.19)
Durable good	-0.18	-0.86***	-0.50***	-0.24
	(0.20)	(0.21)	(0.15)	(0.20)
Year 2002	1.57***	0.41**	0.26	0.64**
	(0.22)	(0.19)	(0.17)	(0.30)
N	430	430	430	430
Wald Chi-squared	328.4***	159.7***	184.9***	169.3***

Note: standard errors in parentheses below estimated coefficients.
*Significant at 10% **Significant at 5% ***Significant at 1%

One result which is consistent across size categories is the pattern that was also observed for the earlier time period, namely that consumer goods industries have higher rates of exit. A finding which differs from the period of the 1990s, however, is that durable goods industries have lower rates of exit. Given the differing industry definitions in the two samples (and the more aggregate nature of the more recent analysis), it is difficult to know the extent to which the changed determinants are entirely the result of the time periods or whether the degree of aggregation is a factor. Analysis at the level of the establishment (using the underlying confidential Census data) would be required to sort these issues out.

While the data suggest that the appreciation of the dollar is a cause of exit generally for import- competing small firms, the effects are clearly largest (and statistically significant) for those with under 20 employees. To get a sense of the magnitudes involved, consider the annual rate of exit for a firm with between 10 and 19 employees. In an industry well-sheltered from imports (say, a 5 percent import share) a 10 percent appreciation of the dollar would lead to less than an 0.1 percentage point increase in the exit rate (around a mean value of 6.65 for the two time periods combined); in contrast, for firms facing strong import competition (say, a 30 percent import share), that same 10 percent dollar appreciation would lead to the exit rate increasing by more than half a percentage point (from 6.65 percent to 7.16 percent). For the very smallest firms (the 1-9 employee category) the exchange rate effects were smaller in the decade of the 1 990s but stronger in the more recent period.

The technology base seems to matter in terms of how small firms respond to these international pressures, especially in the most recent period. Consider a firm with between 10 and 19 employees in an industry with the mean import penetration (combining the two time periods, using 17.5 percent of the mean import share). A 10 percent dollar appreciation raises the exit rate for firms in relatively "low-tech" industries (with the mean company R&D expenditures just 0.5 percent of value of shipments) by 0.28 percentage points during the 1990s; and by 0.25 percentage points in the 2000-2004 period. Relatively high-tech firms (those in industries with a mean R&D intensity of 3.0 percent) are much less affected by international pressures. Their exit rate increased by 0.19 percentage points during the 1990s and barely at all (just 0.01 percentage points) since 2000. The patterns for the very smallest (1-9 employee) firms are similar.

CONCLUSIONS

While results are not as consistent across time periods as one would hope, there are certain findings which seem reasonably robust. One is that international pressures, in the form of import-share weighted exchange rate appreciation, seem to lead to increased rates of exit among the *smallest manufacturing firms*, though the magnitudes of these effects are smaller than sometimes discussed. Conversely, one would expect the current period of dollar depreciation to decrease small firm exit rates. Very importantly, though, there is the strong suggestion that high-tech industries may have been able to avoid much of this impact during the appreciation of the dollar (though they may also not gain much from depreciation). The exact cause of this relationship cannot be pinpointed, but patents and a reputation for innovation may shield a small firm somewhat from lower-priced foreign competitors.

Another result of interest is that consumer goods industries have higher rates of small-firm exit than durable goods industries (perhaps due to the cost and risk associated with establishing and maintaining brand loyalty). Other results seem to vary by both time period and size category, perhaps suggesting that the exit decision needs to be analyzed at a more disaggregated level to account for the complexities involved. Related to this is the important notion that in examining small firm exit, one must keep in mind the idiosyncratic motivations for exit which may not correspond to economic notions of "failure" (as discussed in Headd, 2003). These can play a role in small-firm dynamics, and their impact cannot be discerned in industry-level data of the sort examined here.

REFERENCES

Acs, Zoltan J. & David, B. (1989). Audretsch, "Small Firm Entry in U.S. Manufacturing," *Economica*, 255-265.

Audretsch, David, B. (1994). "Business Survival and the Decision to Exit," *International Journal of the Economics of Business*, 125-137.

Audretsch, David, B. (1995). Talat Mahmood, "New Firm Survival: New Results Using a Hazard Function," *Review of Economics and Statistics*, 97-103.

De Backer, Koen. & Leo, Sleuwaegen. (2003). "Does Foreign Direct Investment Crowd Out Domestic Entrepreneurship?" *Review of Industrial Organization*, 67-84.

Buenstorf, Guido. (2007). "Evolution on the Shoulders of Giants: Entrepreneurship and Firm Survival in the German Laser Industry," *Review of Industrial Organization*, 179-202.

Dunne, Timothy. Mark Roberts. & Larry Samuelson. (1988). "Patterns of Firm

Entry and Exit in U.S. Manufacturing Industries," *RAND Journal of Economics,* 495-5 15.

Feinberg, Robert M. (1989a). "The Effects of Foreign Exchange Movements on U.S. Domestic Prices," *Review of Economics and Statistics,* 505-511.

Feinberg, Robert M. (1989b). "Imports as a Threat to Cartel Stability," *International Journal of Industrial Organization,* 281-288.

Feinberg, Robert M. (2007). "Price Impacts of Small Firm Entry in U.S. Manufacturing," unpublished manuscript.

Ghemawat, Pankaj & Barry Nalebuff. (1985). "Exit," *RAND Journal of Economics,* 63-71.

Headd, Brian, (2003). "Redefining Business Success: Distinguishing Between Closure and Failure," *Small Business Economics,* 5 1-61.

Katics, Michelle M. & Bruce, C. (1994). Peterson. "The Effect of Rising Import Competition on Market Power: A Panel Data Study of U.S. Manufacturing." *Journal of Industrial Economics,* 277-286.

Khemani, R. S. & Daniel Shapiro, (1987). "The Determinants of Entry and Exit Reconsidered." *International Journal of Industrial Organization,* 15-26.

Kleijweg, Aad, J. M. & Marcel, H. C. (1996). Lever, "Entry and Exit in Dutch Manufacturing Industries," *Review of Industrial Organization* 375-382.

Phillips, Bruce, D. & Bruce, A. (1989). Kirchhoff, "Formation, Growth and Survival: Small Firm Dynamics in the U.S. Economy," *Small Business Economics,* 65-74.

Shapiro, Daniel, Chapter 5. "Entry, Exit, and the Theory of Multinational Corporations."

The Multinational Corporation in the (1980s). Edited By David B. Audretsch and Charles P. Kindleberger, Cambridge: MIT Press, 1983. 103-121.

Wagner, Joachim, (1994). "The Post-Entry Performance of New Small Firms in German Manufacturing Industries," *Journal of Industrial Economics,* 141-154.

End Notes

1 Almost all (99.9 percent) of establishment exits in manufacturing firms with fewer than 10 employees are firm exits. (Essentially, these are one-establishment firms.) This figure was 98.3 percent for firms with 10-19 employees, 85.3 percent for firms with 20-99 employees and 29.8 percent for firms with 100-499 employees.

2 Exit rates seem have a post-9/11 spike. In 2002 exit rates jumped for the very smallest and largest of these size categories.

[3] As the dependent variable, exit rate, is a "limited dependent variable" which by definition cannot fall below zero. An alternative estimation approach was also attempted—a Tobit estimation with random industry effects using the *xttobit* routine in STATA. These results were quite similar to what is reported below in Tables 6 and 7. Allowing for within-industry autocorrelation was also tested, with results again similar to those reported here.

In: Global Entrepreneurship
Editors: S. M. Rice and J. L. Steiner

ISBN: 978-1-61209-556-1
© 2011 Nova Science Publishers, Inc.

Chapter 3

LOOKING AHEAD: OPPORTUNITIES AND CHALLENGES FOR ENTREPRENEURSHIP AND SMALL BUSINESS OWNERS

*Chad Moutray**

This paper was prepared for presentation at "Entrepreneurship in a Global Economy," a conference sponsored by the Western New England College's Law and Business Center for Advancing Entrepreneurship, held in Springfield, Massachusetts, on October 17, 2008.

Challenges

The paper outlines five major challenges that small business owners will face in the coming years.

---

* The author is the chief economist and director of research for the Office of Advocacy of the U.S. Small Business Administration (SBA). This paper was presented at the conference "Entrepreneurship in a Global Economy," sponsored by the Western New England College's Law and Business Center for Advancing Entrepreneurship, in Springfield, Massachusetts, on October 17, 2008. The opinions expressed in this article are those of the author and do not necessarily reflect the views of the Office of Advocacy, the SBA, or the U.S. government. Thanks to Joseph Johnson, LaVita LeGrys, Jules Lichtenstein, and Radwan Saade for their helpful comments. Any errors or omissions can be attributed, however, to the author.

- **Strengthening the Overall Economy.** Small businesses continue to struggle in the economic downturn, and it will be important for policy leaders to get the economy moving again. Small businesses will be a large part of that, as entrepreneurs will spur new innovation and employment in the coming years. These firms will continue to be the job- generators that we have become accustomed to. With that said, industries will recover from the downturn in different ways, and some industries have clearly been hit harder this time than in past business cycles.

- **Taxes and Regulation.** Business conditions have a fundamental impact on entrepreneurial activity, and small business owners frequently cite tax and regulatory policies as a concern. Moving forward, it will be important for policymakers to consider the impact of taxes and regulations on small business owners and would-be entrepreneurs.

- **Cost and Availability of Health Insurance.** Health insurance premiums have risen substantially in this decade. The Kaiser Family Foundation reports that the cost of employee-sponsored health insurance plans has increased 119 percent since 1999. It is also well-documented that employees at smaller firms are less likely to be offered health care coverage. Finding ways to control the cost of providing health insurance to employees and increasing coverage will remain a priority for our national and state leaders.

- **Attracting and Retaining a Quality Workforce.** Small businesses must compete for labor with their larger counterparts. This is more difficult in light of the disparity in total compensation, especially benefits, and the result is greater employee turnover. Demographic trends in the coming years might also exacerbate these challenges.

- **Global Competition.** American businesses face competitors on a number of fronts, both at home and abroad. The U.S. government has worked to increase the ability of our firms to compete overseas by lowering trade barriers. There are also some structural disadvantages that work to make our products less competitive, and many companies have reduced their costs by outsourcing some processes and tasks abroad. While insourcing also exists, many of these issues—especially the assertion that firms are "outsourcing jobs"—remains controversial; yet, firms argue that these are necessary strategies for survival in a global marketplace.

This Small Business Research Summary summarizes one of a series of working papers issued by the U.S. Small Business Administration's Office of Advocacy. The opinions and recommendations of the authors of this study do not necessarily reflect official policies of the SBA or other agencies of the U.S. government. For more information, write to the Office of Advocacy at 409 Third Street S.W., Washington, DC 20416, or visit the office's Internet site at **www.sba.gov/advo**

Opportunities

The paper also discusses five opportunities that small businesses will hopefully pursue in the next decade.

- **Increased Investments in Technology and Innovation.** There are strong linkages between innovation and new firm formation, and policymakers fully understand that risk-taking entrepreneurs have positive impacts on regional economic development. With many regional officials seeking the "next big thing" that will drive their local and regional economies for years to come, there is an appreciation that small businesses are leading the way toward new inventions, processes, and products. Such innovations are vital to our economic growth, and they will provide the tools to make our economy more competitive in an increasingly globalized marketplace.
- **"Economic Gardening" and Grooming Local Entrepreneurs.** Proponents of "economic gardening," which has communities plow the dollars that would have been spent on luring big businesses to their town to promote local small businesses instead, argue that grooming existing firms can ultimately lead to greater payoffs in terms of job creation.
- **Pursuing New Markets Overseas.** One of the strengths in our current economic climate is the export sector, and international trade represents an opportunity for small businesses. Historically, many small business owners have not been proactive about trading with foreign partners. While 28.9 percent of the known export value stemmed from small firms, entrepreneurs have yet to fully tap the potential for growth in the export arena.
- **Promoting Business Ownership among Selected Demographic Groups.** Women and minorities have been extremely entrepreneurial

over the past few years—a trend that is expected to continue. One of the driving factors for minorities has been the influx of immigrants coming to this country. Recent studies show a strong connection between immigration and high-technology entrepreneurship, suggesting enormous benefits for embracing these new citizens. In addition, many of the veterans returning home from Iraq and Afghanistan, are likely to devote themselves to entrepreneurship, as previous generations of veterans have done. Policymakers should find ways to promote greater business ownership among each of these groups.

- **Advancing Education and Training.** Education and training are important as there are strong linkages between entrepreneurship and human capital. Moreover, small business owners devote significant resources to training their workforce. These firms are able to increase their labor productivity and reduce their labor turnover. In this way, small business owners should look at education not just as a means of retraining their workers, but also as methods of building new skills, developing new human talent, and preserving employee morale. Failure to do so might result in a reduced competitive position for the most talented employees.

Research Note

This chapter was peer reviewed consistent with the Office of Advocacy's data quality guidelines.

Small businesses play a key role in the U.S. economy. There are many reasons why small firms matter in terms of policy and for our economic health. Small businesses— particularly newer ones in the first two years of operation—provide much of the net new job growth in our economy.[1] Between 2004 and 2005, nearly 83 percent of all of the net new jobs in our economy stemmed from businesses with fewer than 20 employees, according to the U.S. Census Bureau.[2] Moreover, "high-impact firms" account for almost all of the private sector employment and revenue growth in the U.S. economy.[3] As such, it is clear that new ventures are having a major impact on new employment, and it is for this reason that policymakers and economic development officials look toward entrepreneurship as an engine for future economic growth, especially in light of the current economic situation.

CHALLENGES

This section outlines five major challenges that small business owners will face in the coming years. These are (1) strengthening the overall economy, (2) taxes and regulation, (3) the cost and availability of health insurance, (4) attracting and retaining a quality workforce, and (5) global competition.

Strengthening the Overall Economy

The most obvious challenge facing small business owners right now is the economy. Real gross domestic product grew by an annualized 2.8 percent in the second quarter of 2008, mostly due to a sharp increase in exports and increased consumer spending because of economic stimulus checks. Yet, this growth has been one bright spot in an otherwise downbeat economic situation in 2008. As of this writing, we have lost 760,000 nonfarm payroll jobs since December 2007, with losses in each month so far this year, and the unemployment rate has risen to 6.1 percent.[4] Behind the scenes, a series of factors have contributed to extreme levels of individual and small business anxiety, such as rising oil prices, sharp declines in the housing sector, and a weakened financial position of banks and other financial institutions.

For their part, small business owners have struggled, along with their larger counterparts, to weather the economic downturn. The National Federation of Independent Business (NFIB) continues to show that owners are less willing than in previous years to expand their small businesses, to hire additional workers, to invest in new plant and equipment, or to borrow money. In a shift from recent years, their top concern is now inflation (it had been the high cost of health insurance for the past few years).[5] Small businesses have taken a wait-and-see approach to the challenging economic environment, with most postponing the exploration of any new opportunities at least until there are signs that the economy is improving. In the meantime, many firms are looking for ways to streamline their operations or to re-evaluate their business model, paying closer attention to their balance sheet.[6]

For small business owners, significantly higher energy costs affect both the bottom line and the demand for their products and services. In 2001, the average cost of a barrel of crude oil was $25.92; by 2007, that figure had grown to $72.37. By July 2008, crude oil prices had swelled to over $145 a barrel. Today, many would agree that the oil price bubble has burst, with oil prices fluctuating between $90 and $120 per barrel.[7] While lower oil prices are helpful, small businesses must get used to energy costs that are drastically higher than in past years. Moreover, small businesses, especially in manufacturing and commercial sectors, face greater energy price differentials than their larger competitors due to economies of scale, putting them at a disadvantage.[8]

Moving forward, it is important to get the economy moving again. Small businesses will be a large part of that, as entrepreneurs will spur new innovation and employment in the coming years. These small firms will continue to be the job-generators that we have become accustomed to. With that said, industries will recover from the downturn in different ways.[9] Construction and financial services, due to the bursting of the housing bubble, have clearly been hit harder this time than in past business cycles. Construction, in particular, is overwhelmingly dominated by small businesses—over 86 percent of firms in this sector are considered small. This sector has lost 558,000 jobs since January 2007. Only one other major industrial sector lost more jobs in that same time period—manufacturing, with a loss of 587,000 jobs.

Taxes and Regulation

Business conditions affect entrepreneurial activity, and small business owners frequently cite tax and regulatory policies as a concern. Research has shown that marginal tax rates influence firm formation and exit[10] and state-level policies that promote business creation lead to higher employment, gross state product, and personal incomes.[11] Along these lines, we know that small businesses face disproportionately higher compliance costs per employee than their larger counterparts when complying with federal regulations,[12] and the federal government and a majority of states have aggressively pushed regulatory flexibility protections for small businesses when drafting new rules.[13] Other nations, as well, are pushing to reduce business regulatory on this issue in conjunction with the forum; see *http://www.linkedin.com/answers/startups-small-businesses/smallbusiness/STR_SMB/328271-5714444?goback=.srp_1_1222238801916_in.* barriers, as documented each year by the World Bank, and overall business activities in these countries have likely increased as a result.[14]

With these facts in mind, a number of tax and regulatory changes will take place in the coming years, and small business owners will be paying close attention to each of these. At the federal level, several tax provisions of 2001 and 2003 are set to expire after FY 2010, and there will be a lot of debate over which ones will be extended and which should be allowed to expire. Government leaders will also need to address the alternative minimum tax at some point, which continues to affect more and more small businesses each year, and state governments continue to grapple with fiscal pressures that affect their tax policies.[15] On the regulatory front, it is anticipated that there will be a significant influx of new regulations at the federal level on issues ranging from homeland security to finance. As these rule changes are considered, small business interests will need to be thoroughly considered.

Cost and Availability of Health Insurance

Health insurance premiums have risen substantially in this decade. The Kaiser Family Foundation reports that the cost of employee-sponsored health insurance plans has increased 119 percent since 1999, with a 5 percent increase in 2008 from the previous year.[16] These premium increases have forced small business owners to make changes to the coverage they offer their workers, including sharing the cost of coverage with their employees, pursuing lower cost options such as consumer-driven plans, or choosing not to offer health coverage at all. A recent survey by the NFIB found that nearly half of all small business owners shopped around for health care coverage in the past three years; however, only 1 to 2 percent dropped coverage altogether. The report goes on to suggest, "The reason for stagnation or decline in the number of small businesses offering health insurance, therefore, appears to be that the owners of new firms are increasingly reluctant to offer it."[17]

It is well-documented that there are 46 million Americans who do not have health insurance,[18] and many of those people work for a small business. Indeed, research continually shows that employees at smaller firms are less likely to receive health insurance or other benefits than those at larger firms.[19] While virtually all of the employers with 200 or more employees offered health benefits to their workers, only 62 percent of business with fewer than 200 employees offered such benefits in 2008. For very small firms with 3 to 9 employees, the offer rate was 49 percent.[20] Part of the challenge is that it costs more to administer small health plans than it does larger ones.[21] There have been several legislative proposals that would have allowed small business to "pool" together to reduce such costs. None of these bills have passed Congress, however.[22]

The cost and availability of health insurance has long been a concern for small business owners, and prior to the current economic situation, it was their top concern on the monthly NFIB survey for several years. Finding ways to control the cost of providing health insurance to employees and increasing coverage will remain a priority, as well, and policymakers will almost certainly grapple with these issues over the next few years.

Attracting and Retaining a Quality Workforce

Small businesses must compete effectively for labor with their larger counterparts. This is more difficult in light of the disparity in total compensation, especially benefits, and the result is greater employee turnover. Research shows that firms that offer benefits have a 26.2 percent lower probability of having an employee leave in a given year; moreover, the provision of benefits increases the probability of the employee staying another year by 13.9 percent.[23] Firm size is a major determinant in whether a business offers such benefits.

Demographic trends in the coming years might exacerbate the challenges for small businesses in terms of employee recruitment and retention. There are 78.2 million Americans who are part of the Baby Boomer generation born between 1946 and 1964,[24] and the first wave of this group has already begun to retire, a process that will accelerate over the next decade. These retirements pose two problems for businesses, both large and small. First, firms will see a mass exodus of "institutional knowledge" that will be hard to replace in certain fields. For that reason, many businesses have contemplated ways to entice more of these retirees to delay their departure, if possible, but more likely, it poses a challenge for these firms to effectively train others to step into these roles once the retirees leave. Second, the exit of Baby Boomers could lead to labor shortages in some industries, particularly in technology and health occupations. Labor shortages suggest that firms may engage in bidding wars for skilled workers, and small businesses are sometimes at a competitive disadvantage in these. When these positions go unfilled, small businesses are forced to seek other alternatives, such as having existing employees work more hours, leaving positions vacant, or turning down work.[25]

Businesses, of course, have also explored hiring talented foreign workers, especially in math, science, and engineering. The U.S. benefits from having a skilled workforce whether those employees were native or foreign born. There is a lot of evidence that immigrants are extremely entrepreneurial, with one study stating that 25 percent of the new engineering and technology companies were started by immigrants.[26] With this in mind, policymakers need to find ways to encourage the legal immigration of these high-skilled employees, which is currently very difficult to do for both small and large firms.[27]

Global Competition

As Thomas Friedman, notes, the world is growing "flatter" and Americans face competitors on a number of fronts, both at home and abroad.[28] Much has been written on this topic, as the debate over globalization continues to garner attention in academic, media, and political circles. The U.S. government has worked to increase the ability of Americans to compete overseas by lowering trade barriers.[29] Government can also help ensure that trade laws are enforced.

Recently, the National Association of Manufacturers (NAM) released studies on the structural costs of lowering manufacturing costs in the United States compared with its trading partners. They found that U.S. manufacturers pay 31.7 percent more in nonproduction costs relative to the nation's nine largest trading partners. Much of the difference is accounted for in higher costs for tax and regulatory compliance, energy expenditures, health and retirement benefits, and tort litigation.[30] U.S. businesses can effectively compete if they continue to meet the needs of their customers, rely on cutting-edge technology and innovation, and keep their businesses flexible and entrepreneurial (including exploring new markets through exporting).[31]

One way American companies have been able to reduce their costs is by outsourcing some processes and tasks abroad. By producing some inputs elsewhere at a lower cost, firms can more effectively compete on price while focusing domestic production efforts in other areas. To the extent that this practice may be seen as "outsourcing jobs," it is controversial and not without real costs. But arguments can be made on both sides: foreign companies often outsource work to the United States as well—a practice known as "insourcing"—and proponents of offshoring—the relocation of business processes from one country to another—suggest that it is a necessary strategy for firm survival in a global marketplace.[32]

OPPORTUNITIES

This section outlines five opportunities that small businesses will hopefully pursue in the next decade. These are (1) increasing investments in technology and innovation, (2) grooming local entrepreneurs for growth ("economic gardening"), (3) pursuing new markets overseas, (4) promoting entrepreneurship among women, minorities, veterans, and immigrants, and (5) advancing education and training.

Increased Investments in Technology and Innovation

Many economic development officials are seeking the "next big thing" that will drive local and regional economies for years to come. Research shows that universities that invest heavily in research and development tend to inspire new firm formations in the areas that surround them,[33] and governments now regularly promote technology transfer as an important component of economic development.[34] Furthermore, regions with greater entrepreneurial growth have been associated with higher levels of innovation and technology use,[35] and states that promote new firm formation through public policy are more likely to experience higher employment, incomes, and overall output.[36] Therefore, policymakers of both political parties understand that risk-taking entrepreneurs have a positive impact on regional economic development.[37]

These entrepreneurial ventures, especially the university spin-offs, depend on new inventions. One way to track the propensity to invent is through patent filings. A new study being released by the U.S. Small Business Administration's Office of Advocacy shows that 40 percent of the companies that issued at least 15 patents over a five-year period were small businesses. In addition, these small firms produced significantly more patents per employee than the larger firms in the sample.[38] This and other studies show that small businesses are more likely to develop emerging technologies than their larger counterparts. The authors of the new study observe that "Small firms are more likely to attempt to build a business around a new emerging technology, whereas in general it appears large firms work on emerging technologies in order to improve an existing product line or business."[39] This paper goes on to identify emerging industries that favor small businesses; these include: imaging and display, nanotechnology, photonics and optical components, and biomedical and biotechnology pipeline firms. Thus, small firms are actively engaged in the cutting-edge technologies that will shape our future growth. These findings are not new, as they have been documented before in earlier Office of Advocacy research.[40] But it is encouraging to note that they are consistent with past results. A previous study from this office, for instance, found that industries that heavily employ scientists and engineers are "more accommodating to small fast-growing private firms"; whereas, larger production-focused industries tend to have more large firms.[41]

Innovation and entrepreneurship have provided a strong foundation for economic growth in the United States, and the Office of Advocacy has been committed to studying this relationship. In fact, one of the first reports that this office released was a 1979 report from a task force on small business and innovation. Among its conclusions, it stated that:

> "Innovation is an essential ingredient for creating jobs, controlling inflation, and for economic and social growth. Small businesses make a disproportionately large contribution to innovation. There is something fundamental about this unusual ability of small firms to innovate that must be preserved for the sake of healthy economic and social growth."[42]

Nearly thirty years later those words are still true. Innovations are still vital to our economic growth, and they will provide the tools to make our economy more competitive in an increasingly globalized marketplace. Moreover, it is the risk-taking entrepreneur who will often champion these innovations, helping to drive our American economy forward.

"Economic Gardening" and Grooming Local Entrepreneurs

Policymakers eager to show that they are bringing jobs to their district or their state have two options: "economic hunting" versus "economic gardening." The first strategy involves offering generous incentives to lure large businesses. Success can bring a lot of publicity and ultimately a number of high-quality employment opportunities for the area. With that said, not everyone wins at the game of "chasing smokestacks." Some regions will never be able to out-bid others for these high-profile acquisitions of firms and jobs. An alternative strategy seeks to groom existing small businesses for growth. Chris Gibbons—the director of business and industry affairs for the city of Littleton, Colorado, and a champion of "economic gardening"— argues that if communities were to plow the dollars spent on luring big businesses to their town to promote local small businesses instead, the payoff could be greater. Convincing policymakers to think long-term instead of in political cycles, though, can often be a hard sell.[43]

Pursuing New Markets Overseas

American businesses have long sought opportunities where they could find them. For those able to sell their goods and services to new markets, international trade can provide an excellent opportunity. As mentioned earlier, one of the strengths in the economy right now is the export sector. Real exports increased an annualized 13.2 percent in the second quarter of 2008, and these figures have risen steadily, outpacing the growth in imports, since 2005. (Note that the U.S. still imports over $380 billion more in goods and services that it exports; although, the trade deficit has recently improved somewhat.) International trade represents an opportunity for small businesses. Collectively, 239,287 small businesses are known to have been involved in the export business in 2006, the most recent year that data by firm size was reported by the U.S. Census Bureau. These companies constituted 97.3 percent of all known exporters, and they engaged in $260 billion in known export transactions—28.9 percent of the total. While more- recent figures are not currently available, we can assume that small firms have continued participating at the same rate.

Overseas markets can provide new customers for small business owners, but entrepreneurs have yet to fully tap their potential for growth in the export arena. U.S. small businesses have often ignored the global marketplace. Demand for their products and services was sufficient in local markets, and there was no need to enter into the complexities of trading with foreign customers. Size has often been a challenge for many smaller firms, as small business owners could not afford to devote an employee's time to pursuing foreign deals. Research, for instance, has shown that small businesses were generally not very proactive in exploring export markets. Businesses that did engage in international trade often did so based on inquiries instead of a strategic initiative, or by becoming subcontractors to larger firms who were engaged internationally.[44]

Promoting Business Ownership among Selected Demographic Groups

Entrepreneurship has long been seen as a way to better one's self, and research has documented the role that business ownership can play in lifting an individual's overall standard of living.[45] While those pursuing self-employment are varied, studies show that those individuals who opt to become their own boss are more likely to be older white males with greater overall wealth.[46] Despite those findings, other demographic groups have been extremely entrepreneurial over the past few years—a trend that is expected to continue.

Women and minorities have seen large increases in business ownership in the past few decades. For instance, the number of women-owned employer firms increased 8.3 percent between 1997 and 2002 (the year of the most recent economic census), with women-owned firms totaling 6.5 million or 28.2 percent of the total.[47] Over the same time period, minority business ownership also soared, with African-Americans, Asians, and Hispanics seeing the largest gains. In 2002, minorities owned 18 percent of the total number of businesses, and Hispanic-owned firms constituted the largest portion with 6.6 percent of all U.S. firms.[48] One of the driving factors behind some of these numbers—particularly for Asians and Hispanics—has been the influx of immigrants coming to this country. As mentioned earlier, there is a strong connection between immigration and high-technology entrepreneurship,[49] suggesting that Americans should embrace the influx of new citizens to its shores; moreover, where differences do exist between native-born and immigrant self-employment rates, these can often be explained by financial, human capital, and legal barriers.[50]

Another group that will receive more attention in the coming years is the veterans' community, including those who were disabled in service. With the U.S. fighting wars in both Iraq and Afghanistan, many of these individuals will devote themselves to private enterprise upon completing their service to this country. If this new generation is anything like their predecessors, they will be highly entrepreneurial. Past research, for instance, shows that military service is a major determinant of self-employment, and veterans experience higher self-employment rates than non-veterans.[51] One study suggested that 22 percent of veterans in the population were purchasing or starting a new business or considering doing so.[52] In 2002, veteran-owned firms represented 14.5 percent of the total respondent business owners to the U.S. Census Bureau's Survey of Business Owners (or 12.2 percent of the respondent firms).[53] Policymakers should find ways to promote greater business ownership among veterans, women, and minorities in the coming years.

Advancing Education and Training

Increasing educational attainment is one way for us to improve our own potential, but greater human capital also has broader implications for our nation and our economy. For instance, many researchers have studied the linkages between education and economic development, and in general, they conclude that regions with more highly educated citizens tend to be more entrepreneurial and to experience more rapid economic growth.[54] Along those lines, regions with greater educational levels also tend to have reduced poverty.[55] Greater educational attainment means increased incomes and various opportunities. For the purposes of this paper, there are strong linkages between entrepreneurship and human capital. Indeed, there is evidence that baccalaureate education is a strong influence on the decision to become self-employed, and the various attributes of the college experience also play into the employment decision.[56]

From the perspective of small businesses, it is important to keep in mind that small businesses are often the first employers of many Americans, and these workers are often less educated than the rest of the population. As a result, small businesses must devote significant resources to training their workforce.[57] Nonetheless, small firms that invest in training and development are able to increase their labor productivity, and they are also able to reduce labor turnover.[58] In this way, small business owners should look at education not just as a means of retraining their workers, but also as a method for building new skills, developing new human talent, and preserving employee morale. Here again, though, it is worth noting that small firms are less likely to offer benefits to their workers than their larger counterparts; therefore, a failure to invest in training and development could also result in a reduced competitive position for the most talented employees.

Finally, education can also be looked at as a means for promoting innovation. Universities, especially since passage of the Bayh-Dole Act of 1980, aggressively push "technology transfer" programs whereby academically-sponsored research leads to new commercialized ventures in the community.[59] This phenomenon—where innovation provides the linkages for greater entrepreneurship—was discussed earlier, but it is further proof that investments in education can pay off.

CONCLUSION

Small businesses are an integral part of the country's social and economic fabric. Americans have long championed the essential role that so-called "mom-and-pop" stores play in promoting our society's basic values and in our economy. Encouraging small business ownership and new firm creation, though, means more to our economic success than simply the preservation of Main Street values. Entrepreneurship injects vitality and a competitive spirit into our economic landscape that is not readily available from large business. Research shows that small firms play a vital role, for instance, in innovation, regional economic development, and the pursuit of new markets. These firms are responsible for half of our real gross domestic product, employ half of the private workforce, and generate the majority of our net new jobs. Moreover, self-employment serves as an opportunity for many of our citizens to better themselves by taking their fate (and risks) into their own hands and generating new businesses.

Small business owners, though, face enormous challenges in the coming years, and policymakers will need to wrestle with these issues. First and foremost, we need to revitalize our nation's economy, which has struggled for much of this year. Americans are worried about the state of the economy, and in addition to greater economic volatility in general, small businesses must now contend with lower sales, higher input prices, and increased global competition. Reducing such anxieties and strengthening the economic picture will go a long way toward getting these firms back to what they do best—expanding their businesses, hiring new workers, and investing in new technologies to find their niche. Other long-term challenges are equally important to resolve. For instance, small businesses are eager for a business tax and regulatory environment that allows them to prosper without being overly burdensome, and they worry about maintaining and attracting a quality workforce. The fact that smaller businesses are less able to provide and retain the generous benefits of their larger counterparts makes the competition for talent that much harder.

In conclusion, the future for small business in the United States is very bright. Leadership from both political parties embrace policies that stimulate entrepreneurship and its contributions to our economy and to our competitive strength in the global marketplace. This paper has outlined some of the opportunities and challenges that await small business owners. Many of us will be looking to our leaders for solutions to the challenges confronting small businesses across the country. Putting in place policies that promote economic growth and stability will allow entrepreneurs to more easily exploit the opportunities that confront them.

REFERENCES

Acs, Zoltan; J. Catherine Armington. *Endogenous Growth and Entrepreneurial Activity in Cities.* Working Paper CES-WP-03-02. Center for Economic Studies, U.S. Census Bureau (January 2003), available at http://www.ces.census.gov/index.php/ces/cespapers?down key= 101665.

Acs, Zoltan; William Parsons; Spencer, Tracy. (Corporate Research Board, LLC). *High- Impact Firms: Gazelles Revisited.* Office of Advocacy, U.S. Small Business Administration (June 2008), available at *http://www. sba.gov/advo/research/rs328tot.pdf.*

Bates, Timothy. *Race, Self-Employment, and Upward Mobility: An Elusive American Dream.* Washington, DC: Woodrow Wilson Press Center, 1997.

Baumol, William. "Small Firms: Why Market-Driven Innovation Can't Get Along Without Them." *The Small Business Economy: A Report to the President.* Chapter 8 (December 2005), available at *http://www.sba.g ov/advo/research/sb* econ2005 .pdf.

Bollman, Andy (E.H. Pechan and Associates, Inc.). *Characterization and Analysis of Small Business Energy Costs.* Office of Advocacy, U.S. Small Business Administration (April 2008), available at *http://www.sba. gov/advo/research/rs322tot.pdf.*

Breitzman, Anthony; Diana Hicks; Maryann, Feldman. (1790 Analytics). *An Analysis of Small Business Patents by Industry and Firm Size.* Office of Advocacy, U.S. Small Business Administration (Forthcoming, November 2008).

Bruce, Donald. "A Tax Policy Update for America's Small Businesses." *The Small Business Economy: A Report to the President.* Chapter 6 (Forthcoming, December 2008).

Bruce, Donald; Tami Gurley. *Taxes and Entrepreneurial Activity: An Empirical Investigation using Longitudinal Tax Return Data.* Office of Advocacy, U.S. Small Business Administration (March 2005), available at http://www.sba.gov/advo/research/rs252tot.pdf.

Bruce, Donald; John, Deskins; Brian, Hill; Jonathan Rork. *Small Business and State Growth: An Econometric Investigation.* Office of Advocacy, U.S. Small Business Administration (February 2007), available at http://www.sba.gov/advo/research/rs292tot.pdf.

Camp, S. Michael. (Advanced Research Technologies, LLC). *The Innovation-Entrepreneurship NEXUS: A National Assessment of Entrepreneurship and Regional Economic Growth and Development.* Office of Advocacy, U.S. Small Business Administration (April 2005), available at http://www.sba.gov/advo/research/rs256tot.pdf.

CHI Research, Inc. *Small Serial Innovators: The Small Firm Contribution to Technical Change.* Office of Advocacy, U.S. Small Business Administration (March 2003), available at *http://www.sba.gov/advo/research/rs225tot.pdf.*

Chu, Rose C.; Gordon R. Trapnell. (Actuarial Research Corporation). *Study of the Adminstrative Costs and Actuarial Values of Small Health Plans.* Office of Advocacy, U.S. Small Business Administration (January 2003), available at http://www.sba.gov/advo/research/rs224tot.pdf.

Crain, W. Mark. *The Impact of Regulatory Costs on Small Firms.* Office of Advocacy, U.S. Small Business Administration (September 2005), available at http://www.sba.gov/advo/research/rs264tot.pdf.

DeNavas-Walt; Carmen, Bernadette; D. Proctor; Jesssica C. Smith. *Income, Poverty, and Health Insurance Coverage in the United States: 2007.* Current Population Reports, U.S. Census Bureau (August 2008), available at http://www.census.gov/prod/2008pubs/p60-235.pdf.

Eckhardt, Jonathan, T.; Scott Shane. (Peregrine Analytics, LLC). Innovation and Small Business Performance: Examining the Relationship between Technical Innovation and the Within-Industry Distributions of Fast-Growth Firms. Office of Advocacy, U.S. Small Business Administration (March 2006), available at *http://www.sba.gov/advo/research/rs272tot.pdf.*

Econometrica, Inc. *Structural Factors Affecting the Health Insurance Coverage of Workers at Small Firms.* Office of Advocacy, U.S. Small Business Administration (March 2007), available at *http://www.sba.gov/advo/research/rs295tot.pdf.*

Fairlie Robert, W. *Self-Employment Business Ownership Rates in the United States: 19 79-2003.* Office of Advocacy, U.S. Small Business Administration (December 2004), available at *http://www.sba.gov/advo/research/rs243tot.pdf.*

Fairlie, Robert; W.; Christopher Woodruff. *Mexican-American Entrepreneurship.* Hudson Institute Research Paper no. 06-03 (April 2006), available at http://papers.ssrn.com/sol3/papers.cfm?abstract id=90768 1.

Florida, Richard. *The Rise of the Creative Class: ... and How It's*

Transforming Work, Leisure, Community, & Everyday Life. New York: Basic Books (2002).

Friedman, Thomas L. *The World is Flat: A Brief History of the Twenty-first Century.* New York: Farrar, Straus, and Giroux (2005).

Georgellis, Yannis and Howard, J. Wall. "What Makes a Region Entrepreneurial? Evidence from Britain." *Annals of Regional Science.* 3 1(3) (2000), pp. 385-403.

Glaeser, Edward L. "Are Cities Dying?" *Journal of Economic Perspectives.* 12(2) (Spring 1998), 139-160.

Goetz, Stephan, J. *The Place-Based Structural Determinants and Effects of Self-Employment.* The Northeastern Regional Center for Rural Development, Pennsylvania State University. Rural Development Paper no. 33 (September 29, 2006), available at *http://papers.ssrn.com/sol3 /papers.cfm?abstract* id=934636.

Gurley-Calvez, Tami. *Health Insurance Deductibility and Entrepreneurial Survival.* Office of Advocacy, U.S. Small Business Administration (March 2005), available at http://www.sba.gov/advo/research/rs273tot.pdf.

Hope, John, B; Patrick, C. Mackin. (SAG Corporation). *The Relationship between Employee Turnover and Employee Compensation in Small Business.* Office of Advocacy, U.S. Small Business Administration (July 2007), available at http://www.sba.gov/advo/research/rs308tot.pdf.

Joel Popkin. Company. *Cost of Employee Benefits in Small and Large Businesses.* Office of Advocacy, U.S. Small Business Administration (August 2005), available at *http://www.sba.gov/advo/resear ch/rs262tot.pdf;*

Joel Popkin; Company. *Small Business during the Business Cycle.* Office of Advocacy, U.S. Small Business Administration (July 2003), available at http://www.sba.gov/advo/research/rs231tot.pdf.

Kaiser Family Foundation and the Health Research & Educational Trust. *Employer Health Benefits: 2008 Annual Survey.* Kaiser Family Foundation (September 2008), available at *http://ehbs.k ff.org/pdf/7790.pdf.*

Kirchoff, Bruce; Catherine, Armington. (BJK Associates). *The Influence of R&D Expenditures on New Firm Formation and Economic Growth.* Office of Advocacy, U.S. Small Business Administration (October 2002), available at http://www.sba.gov/advo/research/rs222tot.pdf.

Lee, Sam Youl Lee; Richard, Florida; Zoltan Acs. *Creativity and Entrepreneurship: A Regional Analysis of New Firm Formation.* Discussion Papers on Entrepreneurship, Growth, and Public Policy; Max

Planck Institute for Research into Economic Systems (April 2004).

Leonard, Jeremy A. *The Escalating Cost Crisis: An Update on Structural Cost Pressures Facing U.S. Manufacturers.* National Association of Manufacturers, 2006, available at http://www.nam.org/~/media nam/doc s/237500/237456.pdf.ashx.

Leonard, Jeremy, A. *How Structural Costs Imposed on U.S. Manufacturers Harm Workers and Threaten Competitiveness.* National Association of Manufacturers (2003), available at http://www.nam.org/~/media. ashx.

Lichtenstein, Jules. "Small Business Training and Development." *The Small Business Economy: A Report to the President.* Chapter 5 (Forthcoming, December 2008).

Lichtenstein, Jules; Joseph Sobota. "Characteristics of Veteran Business Owners and Veteran-Owned Businesses." *The Small Business Economy: A Report to the President.* Chapter 5 (December 2007), available at http://www.sba.gov/advo/research/sb_econ2007.pdf.

Lowrey, Ying. *Business Density, Entrepreneurship, and Economic Well-Being.* Working Paper (June 2004), available at *http://papers.ssrn.com/ sol3/papers.cfm?abstract_id=744804.*

Lowrey, Ying. *Minorities in Business: A Demographic Review of Minority Business Ownership.* Office of Advocacy, U.S. Small Business Administration (April 2007), available at *http://www.sba.gov/advo /research/rs298tot.pdf.*

Lowrey, Ying. *Women in Business: A Demographic Review of Women's Business Ownership.* Office of Advocacy, U.S. Small Business Administration (August 2006), available at *http://www.sba.gov/advo /research/rs280tot.pdf.*

Moutray, Chad. *Baccalaureate Education and the Employment Decision: Self-Employment and the Class of 1993.* Office of Advocacy, U.S. Small Business Administration (Forthcoming, October 2008).

Moutray, Chad. *Educational Attainment and Other Characteristics of the Self-Employed: An Examination using the Panel Study of Income Dynamics.* Office of Advocacy, U.S. Small Business Administration (November 2004), available at http://www.sba.gov/advo/research/ rs313tot.pdf.

Moutray, Chad. "Recent Research Uncovers Multifaceted Relationship of Entrepreneurship and Local Economic Growth." *The Small Business Advocate.* 26(2), February 2007; 7-8, available at *http://www.sba.gov /advo/feb07.pdf.*

Moutray, Chad; Kathryn Tobias. "Profile of Small Businesses and International Trade." *The Small Business Economy: A Report to the*

President. Chapter 4 (Forthcoming, December 2008).

National Federation of Independent Business. "The Changing Search for Employees," *National Small Business Poll.* 1(1) (2001), available at http://www.411sbfacts.com/files/changingsearchemployees.pdf.

National Federation of Independent Business. "Purchasing Health Insurance." *National Small Business Poll,* 7(3) (December 2007), available at http://www.nfib.com/object/IO 35488.html.

Quello, Steve and Graham Toft. "Economic Gardening: Next Generation Applications for a Balanced Portfolio Approach to Economic Growth." *The Small Business Economy: A Report to the President.* Chapter 6 (December 2006), available at http://www.sba.gov/advo/research/sb econ2006.pdf.

Palmetto Consulting, Inc. *Costs of Developing a Foreign Market for a Small Business: The Market for Non-market Barriers to Exporting by Small Firms.* Office of Advocacy, U.S. Small Business Administration (November 2004), available at *http://www.sba.gov/advo/res earch/rs241tot.pdf.*

RSM McGladrey. *The Future Success of Small and Medium Manufacturers: Challenges and Policy Issues.* Manufacturing Institute, National Association of Manufacturers, and RSM McGladrey (2006), available at http://www.rsmmcgladrey.com/KnowledgeCenter/Downloads/SMM-Report/smm report.pdf.

Schramm, Carl; Robert E. Litan. "The Growth Solution." *The American.* July/August 2008, pp. 35-36.

Shane, Scott. "Government Policies to Encourage Economic Development through Technology Transfer." *The Small Business Economy: A Report to the President.* Chapter 3 (November 2004), available at *http://www.sba. gov/advo/research/sb_econ2004.pdf.*

StratEdge. *Offshoring and U.S. Small Manufacturers.* Office of Advocacy, U.S. Small Business Administration (Forthcoming, 2008).

U.S. Department of Commerce, Bureau of the Census. "Oldest Baby Boomers Turn 60!" (press release dated January 3, 2006), available at http://www.census.gov/Press-Release/www/release s/archives/facts for features special editions/006 105 .html.

U.S. Small Business Administration, Office of Advocacy. *Small Business & Innovation: A Report of an SBA Office of Advocacy Task Force,* (May 1979).

U.S. Small Business Administration, Office of Advocacy. *Report on the Regulatory Flexibility Act, FY 2007,* (February 2008) available at *http://www.sba.gov/advo/ laws*

Wadwha, Vivek; AnnaLee, Saxenian; Ben, Rissing; Gary, Gereffi. *America's New Immigrant Entrepreneurs: Part I.* Duke University Science, Technology, and Innovation working paper no. 23 (January 2007), available at http://ssrn.com/abstract=990152.

Waldman Associates and REDA International. *Entrepreneurship and Business Ownership in the Veteran Population.* Office of Advocacy, U.S. Small Business Administration (November 2004), available at *http://www.sba.g ov/advo/research/rs242tot.pdf.*

Weaver, Mark; Pat Dickson; George, Solomon. "Entrepreneurship and Education: What is Known and Not Known about the Links between Education and Entrepreneurial Activity." *The Small Business Economy: A Report to the President.* Chapter 5 (December 2006), available at http://www.sba.gov/advo/research/sb econ2006.pdf.

World Bank Group. *Doing Business 2009* (September 2008), available at http://www.doingbusiness.org/.

End Notes

[1] Acs and Armington (2003).

[2] The Office of Advocacy of the U.S. Small Business Administration partially funds the static and dynamic firm size data series from the Statistics of U.S. Business. These data typically have a three-year lag, with the most recent being from 2005. See *http://www.sba.g ov/advo/research/dyn_b_d8905.pdf.*

[3] "High-impact firms" are enterprises that have experienced a doubling of sales and employment over a four-year period. See Acs, Parsons, and Tracy (2008).

[4] These numbers reflect September 2008 employment numbers, which were released on October 3, 2008.

[5] See *Small Business Economic Trends* from the National Federation of Independent Business, which is published monthly and is available at http://www.nfib.com/page/sbet. In addition, the Federal Reserve Board publishes a quarterly report, *Senior Loan Officer Opinion Survey on Bank Lending Practices*, which recently has shown tougher lending standards and reduced demand for small firm commercial and industrial loans. This chapter is available at http://www.federalreserve.gov/boarddocs/SnLoanSurvey/.

[6] These comments came from a webinar on small businesses and weathering the economy. It was sponsored by SAP and myventurepad.com on September 25, 2008. In addition, various users of LinkedIn.com provided their own advice on this issue in conjunction with the forum; see http://www.linkedin.com/answers/startups-small-businesses/smallbusiness s/STR_SMB/328271-5714444?goback=.srp_1_1222238801916_in.

[7] This range reflects the highly volatile closing price of West Texas crude oil from August and September 2008.

[8] Bollman (2008).

[9] Joel Popkin and Company (2003).

[10] Bruce and Gurley (2005) and Gurley-Calvez (2005).

[11] Bruce et al. (2007).

[12] Crain (2005).
[13] U.S. Small Business Administration (2008).
[14] World Bank Group (2008).
[15] Bruce (Forthcoming, 2008).
[16] Kaiser Family Foundation and the Health Research & Educational Trust (2008).
[17] National Federation of Independent Business (2007).
[18] DeNavas-Walt, Proctor, and Smith (2008).
[19] Joel Popkin and Company (2005) and Econometrica, Inc. (2007).
[20] Kaiser Family Foundation and the Health Research & Educational Trust (2008)
[21] Chu and Trapnell (2003).
[22] The most recent example of this is the bipartisan Small Business Health Options Program (SHOP) Act (S. 2795), which promotes the "pooling" of health insurance plans for employers with fewer than 100 employees and for the self- employed.
[23] Hope and Mackin (2007).
[24] U.S. Department of Commerce, Bureau of the Census (2006).
[25] National Federation of Independent Business (2001).
[26] Wadwha et al. (2007).
[27] Schramm and Litan (2008).
[28] Friedman (2005).
[29] For more information on small business opportunities and exports, see Moutray and Tobias (Forthcoming, 2008).
[30] Leonard (2003, 2006).
[31] RSM McGladrey (2006).
[32] StratEdge (Forthcoming, 2008).
[33] Kirchoff and Armington (2002).
[34] Shane (2004).
[35] Camp (2005).
[36] Bruce et al. (2007).
[37] See Moutray (2007) for a summary of the Office of Advocacy's research linking entrepreneurship with regional economic development.
[38] Breitzman et al. (Forthcoming, 2008), pp. 6-7.
[39] *Ibid.*, p. 30.
[40] CHI Research, Inc. (2003) and Baumol (2005).
[41] Eckhardt and Shane (2006).
[42] U.S. Small Business Administration (1979).
[43] Quello and Toft (2006).
[44] Palmetto Consulting (2004).
[45] Bates (1997) and Lowrey (2004).
[46] Moutray (2007).
[47] Lowrey (2006).
[48] Lowrey (2007).
[49] Wadwha et al. (2007).
[50] Fairlie and Woodruff (2006).
[51] Moutray (2007) and Fairlie (2004).
[52] Waldman Associates and REDA International (2004).
[53] Lichtenstein and Sobota (2007).
[54] Florida (2002); Georgellis and Wall (2000); Glaeser (1998); Lee, Florida, and Acs (2004); and others.
[55] Bates (1997) and Goetz (2007).
[56] Moutray (December 2007; Forthcoming, 2008) and Weaver, Dickson, and Solomon (2006).
[57] Lichtenstein (Forthcoming, 2008).
[58] Hope and Mackin (2007).
[59] Shane (2004).

CHAPTER SOURCES

The following chapters have been previously published:

Chapter 1 – This is an edited, excerpted and augmented edition of a Small Business Administration Office of Advocacy publication, Report Order Code SBAHQ-09-M-0288, dated September 2010.

Chapter 2 – This is an edited, excerpted and augmented edition of a Small Business Administration Office of Advocacy publication, Report Order Code SBAHQ-07-M-0404, dated March 2008.

Chapter 3 – This is an edited, excerpted and augmented edition of a Small Business Administration Office of Advocacy publication, Report Order Code 332, dated October 2008.

INDEX

9

9/11, 32, 73, 78

A

acquisitions, 91
advocacy, 61
Afghanistan, 84, 93
Africa, 3, 12, 47, 49, 52, 53, 55
African-American, 93
age, 4, 57, 73
agencies, 83
aggregate demand, 73
aggregation, 64, 76
Algeria, 12, 45, 49, 52, 54, 56
annual rate, 76
anxiety, 85
Argentina, 12, 45, 49, 51, 53, 55
Asian countries, 22
aspiration, 8, 9, 14, 16, 27, 29
atmosphere, 20
Austria, 12, 45, 48, 50, 53, 55

B

Baby Boomer generation, 88
balance sheet, 85
banks, 85
barriers, 40, 70, 82, 86, 89, 93
base, 69, 74, 76
basic services, 4

Belgium, 12, 45, 48, 50, 52, 55
benefits, 82, 84, 87, 88, 89, 94, 95
biotechnology, 91
births, 69, 71
Bolivia, 12, 45, 50, 52, 54, 56
Bosnia, 12, 45, 49, 52, 54, 55
Brazil, 12, 45, 49, 51, 54, 56
Britain, 98
Broad Sector Import Share, 69, 71
building blocks, 10, 19
Bureau of Labor Statistics, 62
business cycle, viii, 82, 86
business environment, 20, 38, 39, 43
business model, 85
business processes, 89
business strategy, 29
businesses, viii, 2, 3, 6, 7, 10, 17, 25, 28,
    30, 37, 42, 43, 65, 82, 83, 84, 85, 86,
    87, 88, 89, 90, 91, 92, 93, 94, 95, 101

C

capital account, 40
capital expenditure, 69, 71
capital input, 33
Capital Intensity, 69, 71
category a, 69, 71, 74
category b, 60
category d, 73
causation, 61
Census, 61, 62, 65, 66, 67, 69, 71, 76,
    84, 92, 93, 96, 97, 100, 102
Chad, v, 81, 99

challenges, 1, 81, 82, 85, 88, 95
chemicals, 68
Chile, 12, 45, 48, 50, 53, 55
China, 12, 21, 22, 45, 49, 51, 54, 55
citizens, 93, 94, 95
classes, 73
classification, 62
climate, 24, 38, 41, 83
collaboration, 40, 62
Colombia, 12, 45, 49, 51, 53, 56
commercial, 86, 101
commodity, viii, 59
communism, 27
communities, 83, 92
community, 93, 94
compensation, 70, 82, 88
competition, vii, viii, 1, 9, 17, 59, 60, 61,
    62, 64, 70, 76, 85, 95
competitiveness, 7, 17
competitors, 9, 23, 77, 82, 86, 89
complexity, 3
compliance, 86, 89
conceptual model, 8
conference, 81
configuration, 10, 11
construction, 8, 13, 63
Consumer Good, 69, 71
consumer goods, 61, 70, 73, 75, 77
consumption, 4, 69, 71
controversial, 82, 89
correlation, 61, 63
corruption, 24, 38, 41
cost, 4, 61, 62, 70, 72, 73, 77, 82, 85, 87,
    88, 89
CPI, 38, 41
Croatia, 12, 45, 49, 51, 54, 55
CRR, 41
crude oil, 85, 101
cultural support, vii, 1, 9, 30
culture, 3, 9
currency, viii, 59
customers, 9, 25, 37, 43, 89, 92
cycles, viii, 82, 86, 92
Czech Republic, 12, 45, 48, 51, 53, 55

D

data gathering, 7
data set, 41
deaths, 69, 71
deficit, 92
Denmark, 12, 14, 45, 48, 50, 52, 54
Department of Commerce, 65, 66, 67,
    69, 71, 100, 102
dependent variable, 61, 79
depreciation, 77
depth, 6
developing countries, 3
direct investment, 40, 64
displacement, 62
disposition, 9
doctors, 32
domestic industry, 64
dominance, 23, 24, 39, 42
Dominican Republic, 12, 40, 45, 49, 53,
    56
Durable Good, 69, 71

E

Ease of Doing Business index, 7
economic activity, 5
economic development, 3, 4, 5, 6, 8, 28,
    36, 37, 83, 84, 90, 94, 95, 102
economic downturn, viii, 82, 85
economic growth, 4, 6, 83, 84, 91, 94, 96
economic landscape, 95
economics, 4
economies of scale, 4, 86
Ecuador, 12, 45, 50, 52, 54, 56
education, 2, 9, 27, 31, 37, 38, 41, 42,
    84, 90, 94
educational attainment, 94
Egypt, 12, 45, 49, 52, 53, 56
election, 85
empirical studies, 10, 63
employees, 9, 37, 56, 59, 60, 61, 62, 65,
    66, 67, 69, 70, 71, 73, 74, 75, 76, 78,
    82, 84, 87, 88, 94, 102

employers, 87, 94, 102
employment, viii, 2, 3, 4, 6, 7, 31, 34, 56, 57, 61, 62, 72, 82, 84, 86, 90, 91, 93, 94, 95, 101
employment opportunities, 91
energy, 85, 89
energy expenditure, 89
engineering, 88
England, 81
enrollment, 38
entrepreneurial activity, 5, 7, 9, 14, 16, 20, 25, 27
entrepreneurial aspiration, 9, 14, 16, 17, 29
entrepreneurial attitudes, 9, 14, 16, 19, 27, 28, 29, 30, 31
entrepreneurial economies, vii, 1, 32
entrepreneurs, viii, 9, 10, 14, 25, 27, 28, 31, 33, 34, 36, 37, 42, 43, 57, 61, 64, 82, 83, 86, 90, 92, 96
environment, vii, 1, 7, 9, 20, 38, 39, 43, 85, 95
environmental factors, 3
Europe, 22, 32, 35
European Commission, 33
European Union, 3, 22, 23
evidence, 34, 63, 88, 94
exchange rate, viii, 59, 60, 61, 62, 64, 69, 70, 71, 72, 73, 74, 76
Exit Rate (by Size), 69, 71
expenditures, 69, 71, 76, 89
export market, 92
exporters, 92
exports, 38, 69, 71, 85, 92, 102
externalities, 35

F

fear, 9, 16, 37, 41
federal government, 86
federal regulations, 86
Federal Reserve Board, 61, 69, 71, 101
financial, 10, 24, 38, 41, 85, 86, 93
financial institutions, 85
financial resources, 10

Finland, 12, 45, 48, 50, 53, 55
firm size, 60, 61, 68, 72, 74, 92, 101
foreign companies, 89
foreign direct investment, 40, 64
foreign nationals, 40
formation, 83, 86, 90
foundations, 35
France, 12, 14, 45, 48, 51, 53, 55
freedom, 7, 39, 42, 61
funds, 37, 56, 69, 71, 101

G

gazelles, 2, 10, 29
GDP, 11, 40, 43, 70, 72, 74, 75
Germany, 12, 14, 34, 37, 45, 48, 51, 53, 54
global competition, 85, 95
Global Competitiveness Index, 7, 11, 36, 40
Global Competitiveness Report, 36, 38, 39, 40
Global Entrepreneurship and Development Index (GEDI), vii, 1, 3, 8, 12
global trade, viii, 59
globalization, 24, 27, 40, 43, 89
globalized marketplace, 83, 91
goods and services, 38, 92
governments, 87, 90
Greece, 12, 45, 49, 51, 53, 55
gross domestic product, 38, 85, 95
grouping, 74
growth, vii, 1, 2, 4, 6, 9, 14, 29, 30, 31, 32, 36, 37, 40, 43, 60, 61, 63, 64, 68, 70, 72, 73, 74, 75, 83, 84, 85, 90, 91, 92, 94, 96
growth rate, 70, 73
Guatemala, 12, 45, 50, 52, 54, 56
guidance, 3, 6
guidelines, 61, 84

H

health, 82, 84, 85, 87, 88, 89, 102
health care, 82, 87
health insurance, 82, 85, 87, 88, 102
heteroscedasticity, 72
high growth potential, 9, 10
homeland security, 87
Hong Kong, 12, 45, 48, 51, 53, 55
housing, 85, 86
human, 27, 33, 84, 93, 94
human capital, 33, 84, 93, 94
human resources, 27
Hungary, 12, 45, 49, 51, 53, 55
hunting, 91

I

Iceland, 12, 46, 48, 50, 53, 54
idiosyncratic, 65, 77
image, 31
immigrants, 84, 88, 90, 93
immigration, 32, 84, 89, 93
import penetration, 60, 62, 70, 72, 73, 76
imports, 38, 61, 64, 69, 71, 76, 92
improvements, 30
income, 40
incumbents, 63
Index of Economic Freedom, 7, 35
India, 12, 21, 22, 46, 49, 52, 54, 55
individual character, 28
individual characteristics, 28
individuals, 9, 27, 30, 31, 93
Indonesia, 12, 46, 49, 52, 53, 56
industries, viii, 5, 60, 62, 63, 64, 68, 70, 72, 73, 75, 76, 77, 82, 86, 88, 90
industry, 40, 60, 61, 62, 64, 65, 68, 70, 72, 73, 74, 75, 76, 77, 79, 91
institutions, 5, 7, 33, 40, 85
intellectual property, 40
international trade, 40, 83, 92
internationalization, 9, 34
inventions, 83, 90
investment, 37, 40, 43, 64

investments, 90, 94
investors, 43
Iran, 12, 39, 40, 46, 49, 51, 54, 56
Iraq, 84, 93
Ireland, 12, 15, 46, 48, 50, 52, 54
Israel, 12, 46, 48, 51, 53, 54
issues, 34, 72, 73, 76, 82, 87, 88, 95
Italy, 12, 46, 48, 50, 53, 55

J

Jamaica, 12, 46, 49, 51, 54, 56
Japan, 12, 46, 48, 51, 53, 55
job creation, 2, 10, 30, 83
Jordan, 12, 46, 49, 51, 54, 56

K

Kazakhstan, 12, 46, 49, 51, 54, 56
knowledge-based economy, 28
Korea, 12, 46, 48, 50, 53, 55

L

labor shortage, 88
landscape, 32, 95
Large Firm Expansion, 69, 71, 74, 75
Latvia, 12, 46, 49, 51, 53, 55
laws, 89, 101
lead, 15, 21, 59, 64, 74, 76, 77, 83, 86, 88
learning, 32
legislative proposals, 87
lending, 101
level of education, 9
light, 6, 27, 82, 84, 88
locus, 35
longevity, 33
low-tech industries, 60
loyalty, 77

M

Macedonia, 12, 46, 49, 51, 54, 55
magnitude, 73
majority, 10, 86, 95
Malaysia, 12, 46, 49, 50, 53, 56
management, 6, 34
manufacturing, 4, 28, 60, 62, 63, 64, 65, 70, 77, 78, 86, 89
market concentration, 63
marketplace, 59, 82, 83, 89, 91, 92, 95
measurement, 35
methodology, 11
Mexico, 12, 46, 49, 51, 53, 56
military, 93
minorities, 83, 90, 93, 94
model specification, 72
Morocco, 12, 46, 49, 51, 54, 56
motivation, 42
multidimensional, 3
M-Wt Real XR Change, 69, 71

N

nanotechnology, 90
National Association of Manufacturers, 89, 99, 100
Netherlands, 12, 46, 48, 52, 55
networking, 9, 31
New England, 81
new technology, vii, 1, 10, 20, 30, 37, 39
New Zealand, 12, 14, 32, 46, 48, 50, 52, 55
North America, 62
Norway, 12, 46, 48, 50, 52, 55

O

obstacles, 9
officials, 61, 83, 84, 90
oil, 85, 101
operations, viii, 59, 73, 85
opportunities, 5, 9, 27, 31, 32, 83, 85, 90, 91, 92, 94, 95, 102

Organization for Economic Cooperation and Development, 35
outsourcing, 82, 89
ownership, 2, 3, 6, 34, 56, 57, 84, 93, 94, 95

P

paints, 15
Panama, 12, 46, 49, 51, 53, 56
parity, 11
patents, 77, 90
payroll, 85
peer review, 61, 84
percentile, 18, 19, 20, 26
Peru, 3, 12, 46, 49, 51, 53, 56
Petroleum, 67
Philippines, 12, 46, 50, 51, 54, 56
plants, 63
Poland, 12, 46, 49, 51, 54, 55
policy, viii, 4, 6, 27, 29, 32, 35, 36, 38, 82, 84, 90
policy initiative, 6
policymakers, 3, 82, 83, 84, 88, 89, 90, 92, 95
political parties, 90, 95
population, 8, 9, 11, 16, 25, 28, 32, 37, 38, 41, 42, 43, 56, 57, 93, 94
portfolio, 40
portfolio investment, 40
Portugal, 12, 46, 49, 51, 53, 55
positive relationship, 4
preservation, 95
President, 96, 99, 100, 101
pricing behavior, 64
private firms, 91
probability, 88
process innovation, 9
profit, 63
project, 64
prosperity, 30, 35
protection, 38, 40
public education, 31
public policy, 6, 27, 36, 90

Puerto Rico, 12, 15, 40, 46, 48, 51, 52, 55
purchasing power, 11
purchasing power parity, 11

R

R&D Intensity, 69, 71
race, 22
reality, 27, 32
recession, vii, 1, 32
recognition, 2
regional economies, 83, 90
regression, 72, 73
regression equation, 73
regulations, 82, 86, 87
regulatory changes, 86
relevance, 6, 64
rendition, 4
reputation, 36, 77
requirements, 3, 63
research institutions, 40
researchers, 7, 32, 94
resources, 9, 10, 27, 84, 94
response, 9, 73
risk, 2, 10, 16, 17, 64, 77, 83, 90, 91
risks, 95
risk-taking, 83, 90, 91
Romania, 12, 46, 49, 51, 53, 56
rules, 86
Russia, 12, 47, 49, 52, 53, 55

S

SAP, 101
Saudi Arabia, 12, 47, 48, 51, 53, 55
scale economies, 63
school, 31
science, 88
secondary education, 37, 38, 41, 42
secondary schools, 31
security, 32, 87
self employment, 57
self-employed, 56, 94

self-employment, 2, 3, 4, 6, 7, 56, 57, 93, 95
sensitivity, 74
Serbia, 12, 47, 49, 51, 54, 56
service firms, 4
shores, 32, 93
shortage, 10
showing, 60, 63
SIC, 61, 62, 64, 66, 68, 69, 70, 72, 74
signs, 85
Silicon Valley, 3, 30
simulation, 64
Singapore, 12, 47, 48, 51, 52, 54
skilled workers, 32, 88
small businesses, 2, 6, 65, 83, 85, 86, 87, 88, 90, 91, 92, 94, 95, 101
small firms, 61, 62, 63, 64, 65, 70, 73, 76, 83, 84, 86, 87, 90, 91, 92, 94, 95
social status, 30, 41
society, 27, 31, 95
software, 32
sorption, 42
South Africa, 12, 47, 49, 52, 53, 55
South America, 3
Spain, 12, 47, 48, 50, 53, 55
stability, 27, 96
standard error, 74, 75
standard of living, 93
startup skills, vii, 1, 9
state, 82, 86, 87, 91, 95
states, 86, 90
statistics, 14, 38, 62, 68
Statistics of U.S. Businesses (SUSB), viii, 59, 61, 65, 66, 67
stimulus, 85
strategic management, 34
structure, 14, 31
substitutes, 4
succession, 6
survival, 9, 61, 63, 64, 82, 89
survival rate, 63
Sweden, 12, 14, 47, 48, 50, 52, 54
Switzerland, 12, 36, 47, 48, 52, 54
Syria, 12, 39, 40, 47, 50, 52, 54, 56

T

tactics, viii, 59
talent, 84, 94, 95
taxes, 40, 82, 85
tech sector bubble, vii, 1
techniques, 72
technological change, 33, 36
technologies, 17, 90, 95
technology, vii, 1, 9, 10, 20, 23, 25, 30, 37, 39, 42, 43, 64, 76, 84, 88, 89, 90, 93, 94
technology transfer, 90, 94
Thailand, 12, 47, 49, 52, 53, 56
time frame, 68
time periods, 7, 60, 61, 76
time series, 72
tobacco, 60, 68
Total Early-stage Entrepreneurial Activity (TEA), 2, 57
trade, viii, 40, 59, 82, 83, 89, 92
trade deficit, 92
trading partners, 89
training, 39, 42, 84, 90, 94
traits, 9
transactions, 38, 92
transparency, 38
Turkey, 12, 47, 49, 51, 53, 55
turnover, 82, 84, 88, 94

U

U.S. Department of Commerce, 65, 66, 67, 69, 71, 100, 102
U.S. economy, 20, 61, 84
U.S. history, 30
unemployment rate, 64, 85
UNESCO, 38, 40

United Kingdom, 12, 14, 47, 48, 50, 52, 55
United Nations, 38
United States, vii, 1, 6, 12, 14, 15, 17, 18, 19, 20, 21, 22, 23, 24, 26, 27, 29, 30, 31, 32, 47, 48, 50, 52, 54, 64, 89, 91, 95, 97
universities, 40, 90
urban, 38
urban areas, 38
urbanization, 23, 38, 41
Uruguay, 12, 47, 49, 51, 53, 56

V

variables, vii, 1, 4, 6, 8, 10, 13, 23, 24, 26, 27, 28, 29, 30, 40, 61, 62, 64, 68, 70, 72
variations, 60, 70
Venezuela, 12, 47, 49, 51, 54
venture capital, 9, 23, 40, 43
volatility, vii, 1, 95
vulnerability, 70

W

Washington, 83, 96
weakness, vii, 1, 20, 27, 30
wealth, 3, 30, 93
workers, 32, 84, 85, 87, 88, 94, 95
workforce, 15, 84, 85, 88, 94, 95
World Bank, 11, 39, 86, 101, 102

Y

Yale University, 33
yield, 57, 72